Society, Intellectuals and Cultural Change In the Developing Countries

Society, Intellectuals and Cultural Change In the Developing Countries

Taysir Nashif

iUniverse, Inc.
New York Lincoln Shanghai

Society, Intellectuals and Cultural Change In the Developing Countries

iUniverse books may be ordered through booksellers or by contacting:

iUniverse
2021 Pine Lake Road, Suite 100
Lincoln, NE 68512
www.iuniverse.com
1-800-Authors (1-800-288-4677)

ISBN-13: 978-0-595-41243-3 (pbk)
ISBN-13: 978-0-595-85597-1 (ebk)
ISBN-10: 0-595-41243-2 (pbk)
ISBN-10: 0-595-85597-0 (ebk)

Printed in the United States of America

Contents

Introduction

This book is a collection of articles and a few literary pieces that I wrote in the last few years, during which I was taking up residence in the United States. The articles deal with a variety of cultural, economic and political subjects. Whereas most of the articles address questions globally, they make a particular reference to the developing countries. Even though the articles were written at different times, their contents are interrelated. While all peoples continuously go through the process of development, the term "developing countries" or "developing societies" is used to refer to the weaker and poorer countries of what is termed the South.

Developing countries are facing fateful challenges and are suffering from a low level of development in various fields: governance; policy formulation and implementation; security; education; culture; economy; administration and technology. These countries' underdevelopment is manifested in many ills: a high rate of illiteracy, ignorance, diseases, poverty and indebtedness, corruption, nepotism, squandering and plundering of riches, deprivation, the patriarchal system, degraded women's status, cultural invasion, foreign domination, despotism, oppression and tyranny, intellectual and cultural alienation, little access to modern technology, and antiquated methods of teaching and learning.

As can be seen, these ills and others are the result of centuries-old internal and external interactive political, cultural, economic and strategic factors: they have led and continue to lead to disrupt the natural flow of social and cultural development and weaken the individual and collective cultural personality and characteristics.

Politics is the main feature of human relations. Politics, as defined in the book, is a way to gain and wield influence with a view to achieving certain objectives. With this definition, politics permeates all social relations.

In fact, many of these ills are not limited to the developing countries. They are discernible in all parts of the world. Their spread, however, varies from one people to another, from one culture to another, and from one continent to another. It seems, however, that they are more in evidence in the developing countries.

Concepts differ in terms of their abstraction and definiteness. Concepts and phenomena, including relations, are dynamic: they are constantly interacting, leading to social and conceptual change in the psychological, cultural, economic and ethical domains. These concepts and phenomena are complex, being dynamic, multi-factoral, multi-dimensional and multi-functional. Constant interaction between phenomena and concepts indicates the fault of intellectual dogmatism. As social change is a result of the constant interaction of social phenomena and concepts, then this change is relative to the phenomenal and conceptual factors in that interaction.

An important issue that affects peoples is the role of the educated in the state and society and the nature of the relations between him and those who assume authority, including government authority. Of relevance also for the continued backwardness are the nature of the official and unofficial governing regimes and the role of the political factor in backwardness. Conceptual confusion caused by historical developments and by wrong translation of terms between languages is partially responsible for the inadequate knowledge of political and cultural reality. All of these questions are the subject of the book.

The method adopted in the treatment of subjects and the explanation of phenomena is based on the recognition of the dynamism of human concepts and phenomena. A common denominator of such trends or ideologies as nationalism, modernity, heritage, liberalism and capitalism is the dynamic relationship among and between the components of each trend or ideology—a relationship that rises above artificial boundaries set up by advocates of these trends. These boundaries are artificial and constantly changing, in that they mark the division between differing ideas and positions.

In order for peoples to be better equipped to eliminate their ills and to achieve further progress, their action needs to proceed from the awareness of the pervasive character of politics and of the dynamism of social phenomena and concepts.

Awareness can be achieved through various means, one of which is the application of critical thought. Critical thought requires, among other things, precise definition of concepts and phenomena. Awareness of the differences among these definitions is essential to avoid confusion.

The driving proposition of this collection is that many of the cultural, political and economic weaknesses in the world, in particular the developing countries, are attributable to political despotism, tyranny and dictatorship. From the national and human perspectives, this state of backwardness of the developing countries should be eliminated and a tool needs to be found to achieve this objective. In this collection it is affirmed that the adoption of the political democratization and freedom is valid as an important tool to achieve intellectual, scientific, cultural, social and political awakening; that the establishment and strengthening of civil society are essential for the preservation of democracy; that criticism is an essential means to know the self and reality and to achieve reform and development in various walks of life; and that proper upbringing is just the best means we have for the preservation of cultural and spiritual values.

In the book, masculine gender is used for simplicity, but feminine is implied.

Hamilton, New Jersey
Taysir Nashif
September 2006

Critical Thinking and Its Obstacles in Third-World Countries*

An important characteristic of a critical thinker is the dynamic nature of his/her intellectual criticism; it is a continuous intellectual activity. Critical thought can be encouraged by furthering scientific and literary intellectual creation and freedom of expression of ideas and feelings.

Serious critical thought deserves a more important place in the political and social landscape all over the world. It seems to get scant attention in Third-World countries.

A critical thinker is subject to various forms of restriction. What is a leaven for creation in one place might not be so in another place. There are historical, social, cultural and psychological reasons for not employing critical thought or for giving less attention to it. One reason is that such thought requires a greater intellectual effort to understand it, making people less enthusiastic about it..

Audio and visual mass media in many parts of the world could perform a major role in transmitting critical thought. Those who administer media programs attach less than adequate importance to scientific and critical thinking. This is attributable in part to governmental direction; in addition, the administrators of such programs lack appreciation of the importance of discussing questions related to critical thinking, or are unable to delve into such questions. Sometimes it reflects their conception of the audience's tastes.

The political climate prevailing in any part of the world, in particular in non-democratic Third-World countries, is not conducive to the attainment of full literary, artistic and intellectual creation. The underlying reason for this is political: politics—as the science or art of exerting influence—does not take into account the requirements for creativity. Exertion of influence involves intellectual and emotional restrictions, whereas creativity requires intellectual and emotional freedom and critical thinking.

Non-democratic political systems do not tolerate freedom of speech where it is not in agreement with the interest of those systems in retaining their authority. In such cases, the critical and free thinker may be jailed or even made to disappear.

As a result, critical thought may not reach the public arena and intellectual creativity withers away. For reasons of self-preservation, critical thinkers may mitigate the sharpness of their criticism in subjects and areas where the exercise of critical thinking would be worthwhile.

Politicians enjoy a greater degree of freedom of expression. If they are educated and want to reflect on various questions, they are more likely to be influenced by political considerations.

The gap between the intellectuals and non-intellectuals is a universal phenomenon. Some people face difficulty in understanding critical thought and the way intellectuals treat questions.

Under various conditions and in various places, in particular in Third-World countries, there is a suspicion or fear of free thinking or enmity towards it. This weakens or eliminates critical thought. Such thought fades away and disappears. In many parts of the world, people who are bold enough to express freely their critical and independent thinking are persecuted.

Sometimes scientists, writers or thinkers emerge, with creative and ingenious writings. Yet they are never granted adequate respect or recognition by governmental and non-governmental authorities and the people, and—sad to say—live their lives in obscurity.

Given the multitude of relatively independent social, scientific, cultural and educational institutions in the West, it seems that this phenomenon—of ignoring the creative person—is less prevalent in the West than in other areas of the world where such institutions are lacking or are subject to control by the government authorities. This does not encourage use of the intellectual and critical faculties.

Another reason for the lack of critical thinking is governmental and non-governmental employment, which occupies people with a brilliant or intelligent mind. For thousands of years, state organs have used intellectuals with various degrees of intensity. Intelligent employees still perform jobs which do not require or encourage use of their mental faculty. The prevailing environment of government employment in particular does not encourage critical thinking; it sometimes encourages intellectual laziness. Thus, many discoveries are never made and this is very costly to the nation.

Governmental employees are often asked to implement policies laid down by decision makers. This is not necessarily compatible with creativity. Thus, intellectual creation is subordinated to the requirements of a policy laid down by others.

After passing a long portion of their lives in government employment, these thinkers miss the unique opportunity of a lifetime, the opportunity to experience a burst of a critical and intellectual creativity. Through a psychological process, some of these thinkers may oppose the emergence of new creative talents in others.

Many intellectuals who have not been in government employment covet such jobs. Their creative and critical thinking takes second place vis-à-vis the requirements of government employment; they adjust their thought and attitudes with a view to increasing their chances of filling such jobs.

In many parts of the world, intellectuals engage in university teaching. In some Third-World countries in particular university life does not provide enough incentives to apply and voice critical thinking. In university teaching, intellectuals often subject their thinking to policies and practices of the government authorities in order to keep their jobs and obtain promotion. In such an environment, research and critical study do not occupy a large part of the professor's time; and any research and exploratory thought go unrewarded. Sometimes professors are punished for their research conclusions. There is not enough competition among professors for promotion and attainment of a higher status based on the conduct of research. Researchers might even be ridiculed by their colleagues if they dedicate themselves to research.

Although a critical thinker may play an important role in the life of a nation and the development of society, until today there is no clear-cut, well-defined and recognized role for the thinker in many parts of the world, including Third-World countries.

* The article was published in <u>The Arab American Dialogue</u>, Vol. 14, No. 1, Summer 2002.

Criticism and Creation*

Some people believe that criticism and creation do not meet in one person. This belief, however, is erroneous. A large number of critics and those with creative ability have emerged, in each of whom a great critic and a great creator have joined forces.

In the same critic and creative thinker or writer, the critic may dominate the creator, or vice versa. The domination of one is at the expense of the other, but without necessarily eliminating the other.

In the presence of a strong psychological, mental and emotional state and experience, creation occupies a wider space than that of criticism, and the person of the creator occupies a leading position, whereas the critic retreats. That is because the psychological, intellectual and emotional burst associated with creation does not tolerate the retarding effect commonly associated with criticism. That does not mean that criticism lacks intellectual ferment; it is there, but it is less speedy than the creative burst.

In creation there is a wider space for the worlds of poetry, imagination, philosophy, beauty and magic. In criticism, there is a smaller space for these worlds. For the critic, it is impossible to enter these worlds with the ease and speed with which a creator enters them. When a creator soars, he (and this applies to the feminine gender) can soar very high, and immersed in psychological, emotional and intellectual states, the immersion can be very deep; he dives into bottomless depths. Creative experience moves him away from his world. He quickly recognizes his magical, sacred worlds. He enters with ease these worlds which he sees as familiar to him. The critic cannot cross this space at the speed of the creator. It is impossible for the critic, while observing the rules of criticism, to keep pace with the creator, cruising in the space of unlimited experience. Were the creator to keep pace with the critic, the flame of creative ability would recede, and the speed of the unrestrained creative burst would diminish; the creator would return with sadness from his rosy, violet-like and magical worlds to the world of limitations, controls and routine, all the while looking eagerly back to the worlds from which he exited.

When the writer returns from the kingdom of creation to the ordinary world, the critic in him may return to preeminence, and he will immediately apply the faculty of criticism. But he may feel bored with critical writing, and the creative urge will immediately become active and yearning for poetical, mental and emotional experience. Thus, he would be seen setting out hurriedly the way a lover does toward his beloved one, towards the burning rays of the sun, as if he wants to be burned, as if he wants to plunge himself into the abyss of fire, as if he wants to live through death, and to be revived through entering the unknown.

Whence does the critic derive the ability to reach there? He will not get there unless he undergoes the experience, and at that time he is no longer a critic. The critic in him vanishes, and he then becomes a creator, having no time to waste on that slow-moving, ordinary, familiar thing which is called critical thought. Enduring experience has made him lose the critic in him.

Criticism is more rational than creation: while criticism relies, to a considerable degree, on exercising the mental faculties, the power of creation comprises mind, self, emotion and imagination. Hence, criticism is less free than creation. And, consequently, criticism does not reach those worlds which creation enters.

Criticism and creation may be present in the same text. This might occur at the very beginning of the formation of a psychological, mental and intellectual mood. The more the flowing stream of the writer has increased and intensified in thought, imagination and emotion, the more distant will the creator become from the critic in the person of the writer, and the more the creator will outdistance the critic in the creative burst towards distant and unknown worlds, leaving behind him the critic whose speed is restrained. I do not think that this outdistancing occurs at a certain, definite point; rather it consists in a process of gradual detachment or disengagement between the creator and the critic, through which the creator becomes librated from the quality of a critic; he then explores his worlds with greater speed and with freedom from the shackles of intellectual criticism.

The critic might need some written or unwritten reference works. The creator may not need such works: creation is a forward-looking process, a process of bringing about an unexplored or non-existent thing.

A critic might need to harness powers of reservation, explanation and clarification. He is tied up with the rules of criticism. The hands of the creator are not shackled. He is unconcerned with conventional shackles; they may not exist in his vision. He does not have the luxury to pay attention to them. His creation is unfettered; his world is boundless. As a creator, he is the master of his creation.

The critic needs to be conscious so that he can harness his mental faculties. The creator might not need to be conscious. His own self might burst out with creation while he is taking a nap, or elated with delight, or embracing the sea which embraces the horizon, or confiding in the peaceable moon in the calm of night, or addressing his beloved while encountering sleepiness, or overjoyed with popular songs, or dreaming of a paradise he is looking for, or seeking inspiration in a deserted ancient palace, or pondering while he sees a portrait of the expulsion of Adam and Eve from under a tree in Paradise.

Conflict may occur between the critic and the creator in the person of the writer, when the creator feels uneasy, or when he is displeased or gets impatient with his criticism of his own creation. This conflict might last a long time; the conflict might sometimes calm down, and other times get aroused. It might lead to eliminating the critic or the creator in the self of the writer. The writer might not be able to eliminate the critic or the creator in him. The creator might seize the opportunity of the critic's inattention in him. Thereupon he would indulge in his creativity and return, carrying his creative harvest; at this point, the critic in him might welcome this harvest, or he might criticize it, or it might receive criticism and admiration at the same time.

The writer might decide to be a critic, whereupon he would attempt to still the creative urge. The deciding factor here is the creator's activity, his boiling excitement, his experience, his wonderland and his existence which is looking for a thing which it may or may not know. The creative writer is more zealous for his creation and is more attached and dedicated to it than the critic in the person of the writer. Because the creator venerates creation and because creation is a realization of his inner self, he is indifferent in his creative mood to the critic in his self.

* The piece was published in <u>Dahesh Voice</u>, Vol. 6, No. 2, Autumn 2000.

Politician and Intellectual:
Some Differences in Personality*

Abstract

Components of the human personality interact not only with each other, but also with the surrounding social, cultural and natural environments. Politics is the study of influence and politician is one who seeks to exercise influence to attain objectives, including that of assumption of authority. The intellectual, however, has a greater tendency to approach matters with objectivity.

Relying on observation of the behavior of politicians and intellectuals in the world, the paper at hand points at differences between their personalities in terms of the exercise of influence. The paper concludes with the argument that, given the differences between the personality of the politician and the intellectual, the former is a greater threat than the latter to democracy, pluralism and public interest. It also needs to be mentioned that concepts are taken here as ideal.

I. Introduction

Social, political, psychological, economic, historical, cultural, internal and external circumstances are interactive. They have an effect in determining the components of personality. These circumstances encompass the type of political and social systems—the extent of their democracy, restriction or freedom; and the extent to which these systems tolerate dialogue. Hence, the personalities of, and the relations between, the politician and of the non-politician are dynamic. By study of politics is meant here the study of influence and the influential. (Lasswell, 1958, 13). A 'politician' is one who utilizes various means to gain influence needed to get what he aspires to get in various walks of life, including assumption of official or unofficial, governmental or non-governmental authority. Human personality is complex. Complexity of human personality means that its different components interact continuously with each other and with the surrounding circumstances. Though it has different components, human personality has a dominant attribute or quality. The components are a blend of inherited and acquired attributes. These components differ from each other in terms of the extent of their strength or weakness, depending on such factors as nature and the strength or weakness of the above-mentioned circumstances under whose influence the human being acts. The dominant attribute of the personality, though in constant interaction with other attributes and with the surrounding circumstances, determines the personalities' attributes, attitudes and behavior.

Components of personality include those of a researcher, a poet, a manager, a critic, a politician, an educator, an intellectual and many others. People, whether educated, uneducated, politicians or others, differ one from the other with regard to intellectual depth or shallowness, the narrowness or breadth of horizon, intellectual originality, egoism or altruism, ethical, national and human commitment or disengagement, and with regard to the extent to which their deeds match their words.

Because of the difference in the strength of the presence of the components of the personality of the intellectual and of the politician, methods of their action and of the styles of their dealing with people and things differ from each other.

II. Yearning to Exercise Influence and Authority

The main quality that characterizes a politician is that he has an overwhelming yearning to exercise the most considerable influence, to assume governmental and non-governmental authority, or official and unofficial authority, while this yearning, although it exists with people who are not politicians, is less overwhelming. The stronger this quality in the human being, the stronger becomes in him the quality of politician.

In the personality of the politician, the component of the tendency to benefit from the possible and from the actual is bigger than that component in the personality of the intellectual, for example, and the component of interest in personal matters is bigger than that in the personality of the intellectual; and vice versa.

Because of the difference in the personality of the politician and the intellectual, their positions are also different. Besides his greater ability to decide matters, the politician who assumes authority has a greater interest in preserving this authority.

Given the fact that the politician possesses a greater ability to decide matters, he has a greater ability to suppress the position of the intellectual, if he perceived this position as contradicting his considerations of preserving his authority.

III. Engagement in Dialogue

Because of his greater influence, and his greater interest in acquiring power and in continuing the assumption of power and the exercise of authority, the politician on average is less willing to enter into dialogue. Because the intellectual has a greater interest in understanding and explaining and is driven less by considerations of power and authority than by considerations of understanding, studying, explaining and searching for the truth, he has a greater willingness to engage in dialogue, to listen to the ideas of others and to accept partisan and intellectual pluralism.

Certain factors influence the willingness of the intellectual to accept intellectual plurality, political, intellectual and educational dialogue, and political and social democracy. Some of these factors may be stated as follows: a greater ability to analyze social and political phenomena, and to reach conclusions with a greater degree of calm and objectivity; a greater appreciation of the interest of the society as a whole; a greater ability to separate the subject from the object and to examine the object from a distance; and a more developed trait in the intellectual to derive satisfaction from the production of a meaningful and coherent intellectual construct and formulation.

The politician, by contrast, has a more developed trait to achieve satisfaction through the acquisition of influence and the exercise of power and authority. All these factors are interrelated. They are also interrelated with other factors, such as level of education and whether one's view is more parochial or cosmopolitan.

IV. Tolerance of Criticism and Accommodation of Interests

In the personality of the intellectual, the tendency to criticism is stronger than that component in the personality of the politician. In the personality of the intellectual, the tendency to change or not to change in the light of public considerations is bigger than that in the personality of the politician, who has a stronger desire to defeat his adversaries. The former, on the other hand, has a greater tendency to tolerate those who disagree with his views.

Because of his personality, the politician has a greater willingness to place what he wants to achieve above giving consideration to the requirements of certain ideals. A politician, because of his strong desire to exercise influence and power, has a bigger influence in society and state than that of the intellectual. With this influence, a politician can realize objectives the intellectual cannot realize. Often, the intellectual needs the politician even though he may not approve of the means with which a politician obtained that influence and thereby made the intellectual dependent on him.

V. Tension between the Politician and the Intellectual

Because of the differences in the strength of the personality traits between the politician and the intellectual, and also because of the difference in methods of action and styles of dealing with people and things, tension emerges and prevails between them. And because of these differences, the intellectuals have more reason to criticize and reject the positions and the behavior of the politician than the converse.

Because of these differences, there is likelihood of contradiction between the position of those who assume government and non-government authorities that is embodied in politician and the position taken by the intellectuals who do not adjust to the requirements of the assumption of government authority and to the authority's position towards vital issues. Because of these contradictory positions, questions of intellectual suppression, lack of a free intellectual flow and dialogue, resentment and alienation trouble a segment of the populace and strain the relations between those who assume authority, particularly governmental, and the people. This conflict accentuates the practical and pragmatic elements at the expense of the idealistic elements, and at the expense of giving thought to other issues that, from the people's and state's interests, should receive priority on the national agenda, such as strengthening the basis of society and identifying strategic priorities.

VI. Idealism and Pragmatic Drives

Because of political, cultural, economic and ideological factors, those who exercise government authority give more weight to pragmatic elements than do idealistic elements. The intellectual, being less subject to the influence of the requirements of the exercise of authority, is more likely to be swayed by idealistic considerations.

The intellectual has a considerable degree of self-awareness, of awareness of the people and of humanity, of the principles he upholds and of the history of his people. Hence, he has a greater degree of tendency to adhere to his ideas and positions. This is also a point of disagreement with the politician.

By virtue of their predominant influence, politicians have the lion's share in determining the present and future of peoples, societies and states, and the circumstances of their economic life and security. This gives politicians a significant role. Given the seriousness of their role, it is necessary to curb this power in order to enable various segments of the population to exercise some influence over politicians. This would provide alternative ways of ensuring well-being for the people and the state, and enable the people to criticize governmental and political practices that impinge on the public interest. In this process, the intellectuals have a more significant place.

VII. References

Bottomore, T. B. Elites and Society. Baltimore: Penguin, 1964.

Lasswell, Harold Politics: Who Gets What, When, How. New York: The World Publishing Company, 1958.

McGreal, Ian P., ed. Great Thinkers of the Western World. New York: Harper-Collins, 1992.

Nashif, Taysir. Government, the Intellectual and Society in the Third World. Kolkata: Academic Publishers, 2004.

Taha-Thomure, Hanada. Academic Freedom in Arab Universities: Understanding, Practices and Discrepancies. Lanham, MD: University Press of America, 2003.

* The paper was presented at the International Academy of Business Disciplines (IABD) Conference in Pittsburgh, PA, 7-10 April 2005. It is included in the Business Research Yearbook: Global Business Perspectives. Edited by Marjorie G. Adams and Abbass Alkhafaji. Volume XII, Number 1 (International Academy of Business Disciplines, 2005), pp. 255-58.

The Role of the Intellectual in Society*

A "politician," by the definition adopted in this article, is a person who is actively engaged in politics in order to assume political office and exercise influence. Politicians have—by virtue of their strong influence—the major role to play in determining the present and future of peoples, states and societies, including their economic life and security. Given the importance of this role, it is necessary that various other groups of society should also have a part to play in giving proper direction to politicians, and in posing to them alternative ways of safeguarding the life and welfare of the state, people and society, and in offering criticism of governmental and political practices which harm the interests of the people and society. In performing this function, intellectuals occupy a special place because of their education and knowledge.

Intellectuals differ from each other in the degree of their intellectual depth and originality, breadth of thought, level of altruism and ethical and national commitment, and in the extent of the congruence of their deeds with their words.

There is no doubt that upbringing in the shadow of political despotism, with its lack of freedom and dialogue, has an effect on the intellectual's attitude and behavior. Some intellectuals in the Arab world and outside of it behave in the same manner in which politicians do and which is criticized by other intellectuals. The ego of the intellectual, as with other groups, has its effect in making him less willing to engage in dialogue and more inclined to promote his own interests.

On average, however, intellectuals show a degree of willingness to engage in political dialogue, to listen to the opinion of others and to accept intellectual and political pluralism greater than that which politicians might show. This willingness is the product of various factors, including the intellectual's greater ability to analyze phenomena, to draw conclusions with a greater degree of objectivity; to examine self from a certain distance, to appreciate the benefit to society from the harmony arising from dialogue, pluralism and democracy.

The role played by the intellectual in the Arab world and in the rest of the developing countries is, to put it mildly, not big. That is due in part to the lack of democratization in many of these countries. Arab society is in dire need of the thought of the independent and enlightened intellectual which is propitious to the interests and aspirations of the people. Hence, it is necessary, from the stand-point of the people's interest, that the intellectual play a greater role. This role deserves greater respect and appreciation that it has received so far.

Several factors have hindered the Arab peoples from achieving a greater degree of social, political and economic progress. One of these has been the oppressive and despotic nature of a number of Arab political regimes. In order for an intel-lectual to have a greater degree of self-confidence and courage to express his views, it is necessary that he be free from fear of the wrath and vengeance of the ruler, and independent if him for his means of livelihood.

Those who assume power, of course, want others to follow them, in order to strengthen and consolidate their political standing. In this effort, persons in power attach a considerable importance to certain segments of society, including the intellectuals, because of their enlightening role in society and the respect some people accord to them and to their opinions.

Ethical commitment, with its adherence to values, has an important role in determining human thought and behavior. In the politician's effort to exercise authority, it is highly likely that a contradiction arises between that effort and public ethical orientation.

One of the more conspicuous characteristics of an intellectual is, on average, a greater inclination to description, analysis and the drawing of conclusions after examination, an inclination to stick to his opinions, and to leave a margin of probability of error in thought. The more original and deeper the thought of the intellectual, the stronger these qualities become. Thus, given these differences, the politician's position and the position of the intellectual who adheres to his principles are highly likely to clash.

As the politician in many societies wields more power than the intellectual, the latter often is forced to leave the arena to the politician, who moves with a greater degree of freedom, and is highly likely to behave arbitrarily, contemptuous of any deterrent. Hence, out of fear for his life and livelihood, the intellectual resigns himself to silence or utters a timid opinion, preferring detachment and seclusion, in spite of the fact that the conditions of the people requires that every group, in particular the intellectuals, contribute its opinion on these vital issues. Hence, a significant number of Arab intellectuals live in exile physically and psychologi-cally.

Assumption of power entails control over allocation of financial and other resources, such as the giving of concessions and benefits, including provision of jobs. Thus, those who assume power exert a great influence over the state and society. They can—and often do—deprive the intellectual of the enjoyment of these resources, thereby presenting him with three alternatives: either to stick to his opinion and maintain with much risk some degree of independence, adapt his thinking to the wishes and whims of those in power, or—taking the middle course—mitigate the tone of his criticism.

The intellectual who chooses the latter position may not satisfy those in power but at the same time loses his independence of thought. A case in point is government service. Intellectuals in the Arab lands, as well as in many other parts of the world, often hold government jobs. In such cases, the constraints of employment obviously prevent them from expressing their thought freely, and their intellectual impact on society is affected.

The firmer an intellectual's respect for his thought and principles, the greater the difficulty a politician faces in making the intellectual follow him. Consequently, it is highly likely that intellectuals of this type are exposed to a greater degree of hostility and persecution from those in power and, consequently, suffer financial and other types of deprivation.

The ills facing all societies are many and varied. A portion of these ills cannot be dealt with except by thinkers who better understand the nature of these ills. Persons in power, by persecuting intellectuals with relatively independent thinking, are indeed depriving society of the analytical and diagnostic function which is direly needed.

As we know, in many countries, including a number of countries in southwest Asia, a democratic system is not followed; rather a tyrannical or authoritarian system holds sway. People who exercise power in those countries follow a policy of the carrot and stick: reward in various forms for those who support the regime, with all its negative characteristics, or perhaps for those who keep silent, and punishment in varying degrees for those who criticize or oppose the regime. Most of the best Arab writers and intellectuals have either been co-opted or jailed into silence.

Because of their criticism of or opposition to the government's oppressive policies, some writers' books were banned, and they were stripped of their citizenship and expelled. Prominent Arab thinkers who served as professors at major Arab universities were expelled from the faculty because they had the courage to criticize the regime publicly.

The harmful policies and practices followed by non-democratic governments constitute an important reason why a considerable portion of intellectuals—those who preserve their relative intellectual independence and who do not make use of their thought and pen in the service of those regimes but who also do not express their critical ideas—turn away from political issues, for fear that governmental authorities would harm them because of their criticism of the authorities' policies and practices. This, in turn, harms the interests of society by depriving it of the criticism that might convince government officials to abandon such policies and practices or to change them.

Television, radio and the press are subjected to the control of governmental authorities in many countries, particularly in developing countries, and such authorities determine what is and what is not spread. Thus, even if an intellectual were to decide to express critical views, it would be very difficult to have them spread.

A further constraint on the intellectual's freedom of thought stems from organizational affiliation, which involves commitment and adherence to the positions and objectives of the organization. An intellectual's affiliation with an organization lessens considerably his intellectual freedom, activity and production. Hence, such affiliation harms his role as a promoter of freedom of intellectual exercise and as a person who engages in criticism, creativity, evaluation, guidance and prediction.

A non-submissive, free intellectual can make a big contribution, through his critical views, to pointing out the right political path and the tragic consequences which politicians' policies might have, deterring politicians from undertaking adventures, and reducing the probability that they make mistakes.

The extent to which the politicians pay attention to the intellectuals' ideas and benefit from such ideas depends on various factors. Some of these are the degree of weight which politicians accord to such ideas, the extent of their appreciation of the role of education and of intellectuals, and the extent of the politicians' belief in the importance of paying attention to different and differing views. Another factor is the mentality of the politician. There are politicians who are unwilling to accept others' views, including those of the intellectuals, because such politicians consider such acceptance would diminish their political standing, authority and prestige, and as a testimony to deficiency of knowledge. There are other politicians who have a greater willingness to pay attention to others' opinions.

An additional factor is the nature of the society's culture. There are societies where democratic values such as participation and dialogue prevail; there are other societies where despotism, suppression of freedom, and hostility to dialogue are dominant. A politician brought up in a society of the first type is more likely to show a certain willingness to consider the intellectuals' ideas. In contrast, politicians in societies which belong to the second type do not tolerate ideas differing from theirs. Moreover, a politician weighs the effect of his acceptance of the intellectuals' ideas on his authority. A politician who is concerned that he would not stay in power as a result of being open to the intellectuals' ideas tends to reject them and perhaps persecute their proponents.

In tyrannical and oppressive regimes, the politicians' rush to suppress freedom of speech and eliminate opponents could be curbed by groups of people, including one of self-respecting, principled intellectuals who appreciate independence and freedom of thought, and who do not allow themselves to be used or abused as a tool in the hands of tyrannical governmental authorities, in promotion of their political and economic agendas.

* The article was published in The Arab American Dialogue, Vol. 9, No. 1, August/September 1997.

*Barriers to Effective Dialogue**

Objective of Dialogue

Dialogue is an intellectual exchange in which each participant tries to prove the correctness of his ideas and the error of the ideas of the other participant(s), perhaps before an audience. It is a critical context in which the soundness of views is tested and intellectual responses to them are discovered.

Manner of Upbringing Affects Behavior

The nature of the behavioral, intellectual and emotional response during dialogue is affected by one's early upbringing. The treatment a child receives from parents, family and society may be flawed. He may be treated as mature during childhood; and he may be treated as a small child during adolescence.

These and similar experiences have a cumulative effect on the child's self which continue after the age of majority, and influence how he interacts in dialogue.

Upon attaining the age of maturity, one tries to realize oneself and to rectify the effects created during the first years of life. The roots of behavior, including reaction, are so deep that they make a person pay attention not only to the intellectual attempt to know facts, but also to the desire to avoid having one's argument refuted, which would impact the communication.

Distance between the Self and One's Ideas

Thought has a greater component of objectivity, while the self has a greater component of subjectivity. It is possible, though difficult, to achieve a certain distance between the self and thought. The greater is the distance the stronger is the objective component of thought and the weaker is its subjective component. Therefore, in dialogue, intellectual exchange can proceed farther while the subjective component lags behind.

Putting distance between one's self and ideas may indicate a greater degree of individual and emotional maturity (full maturity does not seem to be impossible). With this distance it is possible to achieve a greater understanding of another's qualifications, experiences and ideas, and to view matters with more abstraction and objectivity, thus achieving a greater degree of intellectual communication.

Impossibility of Separating Self from Subject and Background from Thought

Societies differ in the manner in which their members express their responses. The manner of expression may be more or less objective or subjective, depending on the customs and traditions established in society. There are societies in which members regard dialogue as a kind of fight between two persons in which there are a defeater and a defeated, a victor and a vanquished. In such societies, a person participating in dialogue considers disagreement with his ideas as a challenge or insult to his prestige.

In all societies there are deep-rooted, generally accepted axioms. They are so deeply rooted that people who accept them oppose subjecting them to critical examination. They think that trying to reverse these axioms would constitute a violation of some cherished values. Such axioms control, to a considerable degree, their behavioral, intellectual and emotional responses during dialogue.

Each human being has a psychological, social and cultural background, socio-cultural values, prejudices, biases and emotions. This psychological-cultural makeup has inescapable effects on each person's thought and on the extent to which that person understands the subject of the dialogue and separates himself from subject. It is impossible to have a complete separation of self from subject in human thought; our definition or understanding of a subject is our reflection on it.

Dialogue is inescapably influenced by our psychological and cultural makeup. The extent of that influence depends on various factors, the more important of which are the strength of a person's background and its influence on his thought. A person whose background strongly influences the thought process is less likely to really engage in dialogue; instead, the dialogue tends to degenerate into a clash of personalities rather than proceed in a dispassionate and unbiased manner based on the subject matter.

A difference in political, economic and ethnic backgrounds tends to reduce objective, intellectual communication. The same words, expressions, symbols and gestures can be interpreted quite differently by persons of different backgrounds, thus impeding mutual understanding.

Education and Intellectual Communication

The educational background of the participant contributes to a better and more objective communication. On average, an educated person is more likely to articulate his or her ideas more objectively and weigh the other's ideas in a less biased manner.

Educational parity or approximate parity between participants would be likely to produce a greater degree of objective and effective intellectual communication. This parity or its approximation would lead to a better psychological communication which, in turn, increases intellectual communication.

Specificity, Abstraction and Intellectual Communication

One factor that hampers intellectual communication is the difference in people's ability to achieve intellectual abstraction or specificity. Intellectual communication becomes more effective and objective to the extent that the ideas of the participants are of the same level of abstraction or specificity.

Because of subjective restrictions imposed on human thought, with some issues it is difficult or impossible to reach more abstract levels of thought. Such restrictions may include social and cultural value orientation, ideologies and normative thought. A dialogue participant who has a lower level of intellectual abstraction—and, consequently, a bigger subjective component—faces difficulty accepting the more abstract levels of the other participant's thoughts. And even if he accepts the abstract thought, it is less likely that he will understand it.

Impediment to Intellectual Communication: Different Definitions and Explanations

People use definitions to understand phenomena, whether cultural, psychological, economic, natural or supernatural. What further affects intellectual communication is the use of identical terms that have different definitions and different meanings, and the use of different expressions that have the same or similar meaning. Thus, people's explanations of the same phenomena may differ vastly.

Lack of Listening Means Lack of Dialogue

One necessary condition for dialogue is attention to what the other party is saying. Intellectual exchange through dialogue cannot be achieved unless the parties transmit their ideas to each other. Sometimes, instead of one party giving attention to what the other is saying, he—while the other party is speaking—is busy trying to rally his ideas and preparing to speak. This deprives him of the opportunity to understand what the other is saying. The 'dialogue" becomes a mere expression of ideas by each side, in effect, "dialogue of the deaf."

Ignorance of the Universe

Human society is very complex. Our universe is largely unknown. Thus, it is unreasonable and unrealistic for one to claim a great knowledge of socio-psychological phenomena and the truths of the universe. Given the complexity of human society and our ignorance of the universe, ideas may be wrong and explanations of social, psychological and natural phenomena may be erroneous. Categorical conviction of the soundness of an idea, and sweeping generalizations that leave no room or margin for possible error indicate flawed thought, lack of intellectual balance and seriousness in the intellectual approach to subjects, and ignorance of the comprehensiveness of the universe and the complexity of social and psychological issues.

Human beings need a culture of dialogue, a culture of listening, a culture of understanding each other and views that may be different from our own, a culture of accepting differences of opinion. This culture can be created by several factors, one of the more important of which is education in democracy and citizenship.

* The article was published in The Arab American Dialogue, Vol. 13, No. 1, Summer 2001.

Human Rights: Their Universality and the Means for Their Protection

The human being, who is the depository of the human soul, is one of the finest creations of the One Omnipotent Creator. Human beings are equal at the time of creation. From this stems the necessity to respect them and to enhance this respect. All human rights are inherent in human nature. Thus, human rights are the most significant, valued and loftiest of rights. It follows from this that it is natural for the human being to have such rights in the social, cultural, political, economic and psychological fields. As human nature is of a universal character and is thus independent of geographical and time limits, so too are human rights universal and independent of such limits

Human rights are universal. The source of the universality of human rights is that all human beings belong to one race. As human beings all belong to the human race, it is faulty to have recognition of human rights split geographically, by recognizing such rights for one people and denying them to other peoples in a region, state or continent, or by recognizing the rights of one individual and denying them to another in the same state, just because the latter speaks a certain language, say Amhari, puts on a native African headgear or was born in Nablus, Beirut, Accra or Addis Ababa, rather than elsewhere; and thus split on the basis of color, ethnicity or religious affiliation. It is wrong that a person who was born in a certain Western city should have a greater recognition of human rights than an individual born in Nigeria or the Sudan on account of color. The concept of human rights should be in harmony with peoples' values, cultures and traditions and independent of the level of their development.

In view of the universality of human rights, it is wrong to limit their identification, codification, strengthening or protection to a handful of actors enjoying political, military, economic or technological supremacy. The universal character of human rights is an antithesis to the arrogation, out of biased interests, by any actors, be they individuals, groups or states to themselves the task of laying down standards of protection of human rights and the task of passing judgment on the extent of others' adherence to them.

As human rights inhere in the human nature, they apply regardless of the color of the skin, eyes and hair, of mother tongue, race, nationality, culture, religion, customs and beliefs, and as human nature is one, then human rights are organically connected one to the other. They are interconnected: the protection of one right requires protection of the others, and the violation of one right is a violation of the others. Thus, the approach towards them should be holistic, with disregard of country of birth or residence and of material conditions. Being natural, human rights are of ancient origin and existed prior to international conventions and other instruments relating to human rights and formulated over the past few decades.

As human rights are inherent in human nature, it is necessary to take effective and all-embracing measures to encourage their realization and protection at various levels and in various fields. Among those rights are cultural, moral, political, civic and economic rights. They include the right to life and happiness, the right to enjoy dignity, the rights of children and women, the right of the handicapped to be fully integrated into society, the right to social, cultural and economic development, the right to enjoy social, economic and judicial justice, the right of indigenous people and of ethnic, religious and linguistic minorities to protection and equality, the right to a minimum of material and psychological well-being, the right to education, the right to enjoy freedom, including freedom from fear and want and freedom of speech, the right of ownership of the homeland, of the land of birth, upbringing and residence. People have sovereignty over their homeland, over its fate and riches. This sovereignty is an inalienable right.

The exercise of the faculty of thinking is a natural human right. A quality of thinking is that it is a tool which the human being uses in the performance of functions. One of these functions is to know his social and natural environments. This knowledge greatly helps the human being in preserving his existence and survival, hence man's natural right to exercise thinking. As the human being is in existence, it is natural that he seeks to maintain that existence or survival. Given the fundamental importance of thinking, it is tragic for the human being to have his ability to think destroyed and to have him stripped of this right.

Various individuals, groups, governments and states have destroyed and continue to destroy man's faculty of thinking. This destruction is driven by various political, economic and ideological considerations. A stronger group or government has the ability to suppress the thinking faculty of weaker groups. Domestic and foreign sources of power have a strong legacy in various fields in the developing countries. Perhaps the most dangerous aspect of this legacy has been the suppression of the thinking faculty of the developing peoples.

Human societies, particularly third-world societies, still witness attempts by governmental and non-governmental authorities to destroy the thinking faculty of those individuals who in actuality have the status of subjects and who are deprived of the status of citizens, and who have no strength to cope with the tyranny and aggression of those few who are at the helm of power.

Given the natural character of the human right to use the faculty of thinking, no individual, group, government or state has the right to suppress or to try to suppress this faculty. As this right is natural, it has a priority over positive laws.

Individuals differ one from the other in the extent of their tendency or lack of it to try to suppress the thinking faculty of other individuals. This difference is attributable to various factors. Tolerance in this field is promoted by an upbringing that respects for others' rights and gives consideration to the natural and social limits that are valid or supposed to be valid among human beings. Also included is awareness of the meaning of good citizenship and of the importance of preserving good relations for the protection of society and of preserving the interests of its individuals.

States differ in the extent of their tendency to suppress the thought of people. This difference depends on various factors, such as whether the form of government is democratic or tyrannical, a majority or a minority rule, on the extent of the power of individuals and groups in the economic and organizational fields in the state, the extent of the economic independence of individuals from the state authorities, on the extent of the appreciation of those who wield government authority of the importance of intellectual freedom, and on the extent of their awareness of the sanctity, naturalness and inviolability of human rights.

Societies, particularly those of Asia, Africa and Latin America, that have been exhausted by cruel foreign social, economic, and political domination face complex challenges. This requires availability of the opportunity for all members of society to exercise the faculty of thinking in order to bring forth concepts and proposals to confront challenges. This opportunity is better than having the exercise limited to a number of individuals and groups, or to those who wield authority, or to a certain social segment. People, whether individuals or groups, have motives and considerations when dealing with issues. The availability of this opportunity makes it possible to know more dimensions of the issues, thereby facilitating the reaching of more correct ways to cope with the issues under consideration.

These forms of freedom are a source of strength for the individual, people and the state. Individuals who lack intellectual independence, follow others intellectually and lack other forms of freedom are vulnerable. Such individuals do not possess the power to manage their life affairs and to preserve their rights and survival. A state and people cannot be strong if the individual members of society lack intellectual freedom and independence.

Social, political and economic progress, to which peoples aspire, cannot be realized without the achievement of intellectual freedom, as intellectual restriction eliminates the possibility of intellectual creativity necessary for the achievement of progress. This achievement requires the intellectual ability to cope with the complex conditions which prevent developing peoples from forging ahead with their life, and to diagnose and cure their ills. This intellectual ability is not available in the absence of favorable conditions for intellectual freedom.

What contradicts the universality of human rights is the selectivity of their exercise, and the resort to them according to the benefit one derives, guided by foreign-policy objectives and economic and strategic interests. Human rights are not upheld when the right to economic development can be exercised but the right to express one's opinion cannot. Exercise of one right does not render unnecessary the exercise of another. Human rights and the value of the human being inherent in them are so important that it would be grossly immoral to subject them to political considerations and interests, or to use them as a means for political, cultural or economic pressure or for maintaining oppressive military, occupying or racist regimes in power. To do so would show the hypocrisy of those who pay lip service to respect for human rights and who, in the meantime, violate them. To confine the realization of these rights to certain categories of people would mean that such rights are not universal. The adoption of a double standard would mean encroachment on the universality of these rights.

As a human right, economic development is very much connected to human dignity, and should therefore be held sacred. It should be a priority on the governmental agenda. It is necessary to avoid giving priority to political rights over social and economic rights. Human rights cannot be enjoyed when people are deprived of food, clothing, shelter, education, health, medical care and employment opportunities.

To strengthen respect for human rights, the rule of law should be upheld and democracy should be exercised within this framework. There is an inseparable and organic link between human rights and democracy. Political rights, including the right to enjoy freedom, justice and expression of opinion, cannot be realized without democratization. At the same time, democracy cannot be maintained without achieving a minimum level of economic sufficiency for peoples. Poverty, which is the lot of a great majority of the world's peoples, constitutes an impediment to the spread of democracy and, consequently, to the protection of human rights. In the case of the inhumane social conditions suffered by billions of people in Asia, Africa and Latin America, the right to development is meaningless.

There is an inseparable and organic link between human rights and socio-economic development. Many human rights cannot be realized without the achievement of growth and development.

Furthermore, the realization of human rights is dependent on social harmony. Protection of the more vulnerable groups in society, such as women, children, the handicapped and linguistic, religious and ethnic minorities, is essential to human rights. The realization of their rights leads to political and social stability and harmony.

Today, there are formidable challenges to the guarantee of respect for the human rights of hundreds of millions of human beings in many parts of the world. It is the responsibility of the individual, the state and the international community to act diligently for the protection of these rights.

Questions of peace, security and war are inseparable from respect for human rights. Wherever human rights are respected, the outbreak of war is less likely and the achievement of peace and security is more likely. Recognition of human rights is one thing; guarantee of the exercise of these rights is another.

In its resolution 45/155, the UN General Assembly, during its forty-fifth regular session, called for the convening of a world conference to address issues related to the promotion and protection of human rights. The conference, held in Vienna in June 1993, provided a propitious opportunity for the international community to assess its achievements and failures in the field of human rights during the quarter century that had elapsed since the first such conference, held in Teheran in 1968. The Vienna Conference addressed fundamental issues, such as respect for the cultural, religious and ethical values of all nations, the indivisibility of human rights, and rejection of selectivity, double standards and manipulation in the field of human rights. The final document that the conference adopted contained a declaration and a programme of action. With its emphasis on the universality of human rights and their indivisibility, the adoption of this document represented a movement towards the strengthening of such rights.

Certain paths taken, such as democratization and pluralism, support human rights and strengthen their observance. Social, political and economic suppression restricts human creativity, which thrives on intellectual and emotional freedom. A society dominated by suppression lacks democracy, which should be predicated on pluralism. Pluralism means making available the opportunity for realizing intellectual alternatives in the various fields of human activity.

Creativity is strongly dependent on democracy, under the aegis of which the human being has a greater degree of intellectual freedom, a greater opportunity to express his views, an enhanced feeling of security and more courage to direct criticism and to express views that call for change or correction and to put forward new, daring and unrestricted ideas. All these factors must be available if the human being is to be intellectually and artistically creative.

There is no democracy in the absence of political, social and economic pluralism; this pluralism opens the way to intellectual alternatives in the various fields of life.

For human society to be free, its individuals must be brought up with a willingness to listen and engage in dialogue with each other. Freedom of expression cannot be achieved without the elimination of fear of the consequences of expressing different and even contradictory views. Thought is enhanced through intellectual freedom; exercise of this freedom through discussion and dialogue enriches and invigorates thought.

Democracy plays a very important role in safeguarding peace and security: it is a tool that enables the majority of voters to decide on issues that concern all the citizens. Clearly, decisions on vital issues, if taken by the majority, rest on a sounder basis and enjoy wider acceptance, and these issues include peace and security.

There are links between social, psychological, political, cultural, economic and artistic forms of freedom; they influence each other. Political freedom, for example, cannot be realized in the absence of the other forms of freedom.

In the democratic social framework, interaction takes place between governmental objectives, on the one hand, and social, economic and cultural interests, on the other. If the two categories come into conflict, when officials and decision-makers stress their governmental considerations without regard for other interests—and maybe suppress them—then those governmental considerations are imposed on society. In this way, society becomes stripped of democracy. If freedom in the economic, cultural, social and artistic fields is suppressed or neglected, governmental practices are divorced from the prevailing values in these fields and are imposed on the social reality, thereby negating democracy. As noted in a preceding section of this article, democracy provides the opportunity to realize different intellectual alternatives.

Discussion of the issue of human rights and of forms of freedom is bound to give rise to the question of the line that separates them from the public interest.

This question, which has received much attention in social and philosophical thought for at least the past three thousand years, does not yet seem to have been resolved. The peoples of the world aspire to social, economic, political and technological progress. The primary motives for this aspiration are the preservation of the material and cultural existence of these peoples and the realization of their economic welfare and social and national security.

To achieve progress, various conditions need to be met, at the head of which lie the exercise of human rights and realization of the various forms of freedom.

One of the functions of the state and society is to protect the individual's natural rights and freedoms insofar as their exercise does not affect the public interest. A very relevant question is what is the line separating the exercise of individual rights and the public interest? Who draws this line? To answer these questions, the public interest needs to be identified and defined. It consists of the group of ideals, values, goals and interests of the people. The overall worth of this group to society determines the balance to be struck between the exercise of rights and freedoms, on the one hand, and the restriction of this exercise, on the other.

In fact, the answer to this question is more complex than it initially seems. It is very difficult or even impossible to precisely determine the location of the dividing line because the components of public interest, as well as the definition of human rights and freedoms, are subject to varying objective and subjective interpretations, and driven by varying motives and considerations.

In societies in general, there is agreement on some ideals, objectives, values and interests, and disagreement on others. These disagreements are embodied in the emergence of different currents, such as secular, religious, national and capitalist ones. It needs to be mentioned in this context, however, that these currents are not mutually exclusive and at some points they converge. Almost all of them incorporate the view that there is a need for protection of the homeland, self-defense and respect for human dignity.

So long as this group has not been determined, there are various interpretations, readings, considerations and disagreements among the various currents regarding the identity of its components. Hence, from the viewpoint of free thinking, it is impossible to draw a line separating the exercise of natural individual rights and freedoms, on the one hand, and the requirements of preserving the ideals and interests of the public, on the other.

Humanity and Civilization

Humanity is the care for the totality of human beings. Hence, exclusivity—which in the context of the care for humanity is care for only a certain proportion of human beings—is not humanity. Racism, which is preference for certain human beings or groups, or which holds them superior on the grounds of genetics or heredity, is not—and is against—humanity, as humanity does not make differentiation, on this basis, among the members of the single human race. Racism is exclusivist; as such it is far away from humanity. Whereas humanity is consideration for the totality of the human race, racism is consideration for part of that totality. Humanity is superior to racism as totality or universality is superior to partiality and exclusivity. Whereas totality is completeness, hence perfect, partiality is incompleteness, hence imperfect.

We human beings belong, as the description denotes, to the totality of humanity not by virtue of the color of our skin, eyes and hair. These are not the properties specific to humanity, as non-human creatures do exist with color of skin, eyes or hair similar to those of human beings. It is the spirit in us, whose fundamental attributes are a highly developed sensitive and intellectual capacity, which has differentiated us from the rest of creation, which has determined our belonging to the human totality, and which has characterized us as human beings. The human spirit, which has a tendency to freedom, emancipation and innovation, has a mastery over the human totality.

No one ethnic group can claim monopoly on making contribution to civilization. Communities from all continents and seas, from times immemorial throughout human history up to the present day, have contributed to human civilization. Asian, African, European, Oceanic, and pre- and post-1492 American peoples have made human civilization, embodied in intellectual contributions which are historically significant for the human race and relevant to its progress.

Human beings should be grateful to the Almighty for occasioning the existence of human beings at the same time on one planet, as this co-existence should and could be an inexhaustible source of intellectual innovation and enrichment for the benefit of all human beings.

It is a mark of shortsightedness and vanity for advocates of ethnic superiority to determine the inequality of members of the human race by virtue of the technological and scientific discoveries which were accomplished in the last two centuries. This thinking is shortsighted and vain because it does not take account of the intellectual contributions by other peoples, for instance, by non-Europeans, in the many centuries of pre-Renaissance history. These contributions, coming as they did before the more recent contributions, and in many cases starting from modest beginnings or even from scratch, are no less, and may be more important, than the intellectual contributions which were made later. This thinking is also shortsighted and vain because, by passing judgment on the intellectual capacity of peoples over a relatively short period of time in the human existence—say, two or three centuries—as proponents of ethnic superiority do, is an arbitrary limitation of the span of human time or an arbitrary limitation of the yardstick by which human intellectual capacity is measured.

Human civilization did not start with the fifteenth-century European Renaissance. Nor did it start with the earlier Greek philosophical and scientific legacy; nor was it begun with the Arab and Muslim scientific and philosophical contributions. These contributions were preceded by ancient Mesopotamian, Egyptian-African, Indian, Chinese and other tributaries of human thought and knowledge. These and other sources make up human civilization in its totality and entirety as we have come to know it. Individuals belonging to various ethnic groups have discovered astronomy, astrology, the infinity and systemic order of the cosmos, biology, optics, chemistry, agriculture, medicine, algebra (the very word was taken from Arabic), mathematics, engineering, architecture, geometry, military strategy and tactics, tools of scientific research, terms such as objectivity, subjectivity, value-freedom, value-orientation, and many more long before the European Renaissance.

To be scientific is, inter alia, to be consistent in the application of the methods of scientific discovery and in the understanding of natural and human, including social, phenomena. To be scientific is to explain, namely, identify causal relations between, phenomena. To theorize is to reach higher levels of generalizations based on the establishment of causal relations. There are historical factors which explain the miserable conditions prevailing in the developing countries. One of the most important factors is the

European, then Western, economic, military and political influence on these countries. This influence has contributed tremendously to the prevention of these countries from extricating themselves from their economic and social miseries, and from taking the course of social, economic and technological progress and development.

The ego-centric, self-centered, short-sighted and shallow view of exponents of ethnic superiority is not and will not help those who approach other human beings in terms of racial superiority and ethnic affiliation to understand, assuming that they wish to understand (and maybe they do not) the underlying factors for the developing countries' lagging behind, in the economic and technological fields and not in the field of human and humane values, and for the contemporary Western achievements in sciences and technology. This lagging behind and this achievement are not, as the advocates of racial superiority tend or like to believe, the result of non-European mental or intellectual inferiority and European intellectual superiority. What can make those advocates understand these factors is to take a more balanced and objective view of human development and history as a product of the interplay and interaction of the social, military, economic and political variables which have shaped the development of human societies, and which have allowed, to varying degrees, human beings to contribute their share of human civilization.

Protection of Civilians in Armed Conflicts, With Particular Reference to Children*

An abstract

Innocent civilian populations are deliberately and indiscriminately targeted on political, ethnic and religious grounds by combatants in armed conflicts. The situation of children is the worst. To protect civilians, international humanitarian law needs to be enforced, perpetrators of crime against civilians should be brought to justice, the concept of peace should be broadened so that it can address social and economic problems, which lead to conflict, and flow of arms across state boundaries must be curbed, cooperation between UN organs, in particular the General Assembly and the Security Council, and other international and national organizations should be strengthened and humanitarian action needs to be depoliticized.

Introduction

Over 20 open conflicts are raging today the world over, in many of which innocent civilians, especially women, children, the sick and elderly and the personnel of humanitarian agencies, are deliberately and indiscriminately targeted with growing frequency for genocide on political, ethnic and religious grounds by combatants. Many innocent civilians have also been victims of anti-personnel landmines. What is most disturbing is the increasing "civilianization" of conflict itself. The enemy is identified with a different religious, ethnic or linguistic minority or simply with the members of a different group.

Civilians have suffered in conflicts in which the most reprehensible means have been and are still being used against them. Cruel and degrading treatment, psychological and physical torture, killing and mutilation of civilians are well-known characteristics of these conflicts. Human suffering as a result is on the increase.

These attacks on innocent civilian populations clearly violate the norms and principles of international law, including international humanitarian and human rights laws, such as the 1949 Geneva Convention Relative to the Protection of Civilian Persons in Time of War. Such attacks deserve a strong and resolute response by the international community. The perpetrators must account for their crimes with the appropriate punishment.

The paper at hand sets as its goal to discuss legal, political and economic ways to protect civilians, in particular children, in armed conflicts. United Nations sources, including records of the meetings of the Security Council and the General Assembly during the last three years, served as a basis for this discussion.

Maintaining of a Proper Historical Perspective

Targeting of civilians in armed conflicts is not a novel phenomenon. There is a voluminous amount of published literature from various sources which indicates that serious humanitarian abuses were perpetrated throughout history. However, sources have pointed out that, out of the estimated 22 million people who died in armed conflicts since 1945, about one quarter died in the 1990s, and that, while at the beginning of the 20th century 85 to 90 per cent of war deaths were soldiers, near the end of the century 75 per cent, on average, are civilians. According to other sources, in World War I civilians accounted for only 5 per cent of casualties. In World War II civilian casualties increased to 48 per cent. (1)

Threats to peace have come both from conflicts between states and from internal or ethnic conflicts involving irregular forces, including autonomous armed elements, some of which neither answer to a unified command nor respect international law on human rights. Given the interplay of strategic, political, military and economic factors on the domestic and international scenes, it is impossible to categorize conflicts as taking place between states or as internal and ethnic conflicts. Put differently, it is not possible to delineate between inter-state and intra-state conflicts. In many so-called internal conflicts, states had a leading role in igniting them.

Related to the proper labeling of conflicts with the view to have a proper perspective of reality is the need to avoid use of euphemisms in describing facts. Things must be called by their real names. Some sources refer to many conflicts as "humanitarian crises" or "humanitarian disasters." But conflicts are much more than that. Whereas "humanitarian disasters" or "humanitarian crises" may be other than political, "conflict" is political in character. Labeling "conflicts" with such labels is highly likely to distract the attention of the international community from aspects of the conflict which need to be addressed not in terms of humanitarian assistance but in political terms. The political aspect must be dealt with in political terms. When there is politics in a situation there would certainly be social and economic implications of that situation. Since such implications have their political origins, they can be addressed only in political terms.

Children

Of the civilian population, the situation of children is the worst. A high percentage of civilian victims are children. The statistics of displaced children are alarming. Of the nearly 25 million refugees and internally displaced persons, 80 per cent are women and children. (2) More than half the total population of displaced persons—both those displaced within their national boundaries and those who have crossed national boundaries—are children. Over 13 million children are internally displaced and made homeless. Those who manage to escape the attacks of combatants often have no place to shelter. Many of them are trapped in highly militarized environments, found in camps for refugees and for the internally displaced, where women and children are especially vulnerable to sexual assault and violence, and boys to forced recruitment. They are struck by landmines and are either killed or maimed for life. In the course of the last decade, more than two million children have been killed in conflicts, more than one million have been orphaned, and more than six million have been permanently or seriously injured. And, indeed, some of the worst forms of trauma and violation—rape and other forms of sexual violence—are routinely committed against women, especially young women, in situations of conflict. More than 10 million are estimated to be suffering from grave emotional and psychological trauma.

Additionally, children are increasingly recruited and deployed as soldiers and killers or pressed into service as porters and sexual slaves. Others are abducted. Some join just to survive. Some of these children are less than 10 years old. Over 300,000 children, both boys and girls, have taken part as combatants in the 30 most recent conflicts. Many of the reasons for children's participation in armed conflicts are often the very reasons for the conflicts themselves: marginalization, discrimination, poverty and displacement. Girls are traumatized through rape. They become instant mothers, either by having to assume the role of parenthood because their parents have been killed or by being forced to bear children.

The children's situation is particularly sensitive, because they are vulnerable during conflicts and because their post-conflict social, economic and psychological rehabilitation is complex.

Recruitment and deployment of child soldiers who are often orphans of the same conflict is absurd, for they become cruel and as such take vengeance against their opponents. Hatred and enmity are inculcated in them, and unless measures are taken to stop this practice, it will be disastrous for societies with this kind of soldiers.

Ways to Protect Civilians

Because of the nature of the protection of civilians in armed conflict, cooperation and coordination of the work of such organs as the UN General Assembly, the Security Council, the Economic and Social Council, UNESCO and others need to be strengthened. This would involve information exchange among these organs. Because of the nature of the protection of civilians in armed conflicts, the approach should be multi-dimensional. Comprehensiveness of approach should be understood not only as having horizontal dimensions, but also as having vertical dimensions, including the need to address the root causes of conflict. It should cover the legal, political, economic, social, military and humanitarian dimensions. In the view of the representative of Canada in his statement before the UN Security Council: "The ultimate aim of the Council's work is to safeguard the security of the world's people, not just the States in which they live. Faced with the disproportionate toll that modern conflict takes on civilians, the protection of individuals should be a primary consideration in the Council's activities." (3) He expressed the view that active Council engagement would eliminate the power vacuum and would also reinforce the legitimacy of the states. He pointed out that it is the prerogative and the obligation of states to ensure the protection of all citizens, especially in times of armed conflicts. As a consequence of failed states or weakened state structures or for some other reasons, governments sometimes do not or cannot provide much protection. In these cases, Security Council action to defend civilians in armed conflicts would, in the Canadian view, reduce the threat to the states themselves.

A number of states, in particular Western states, associated themselves with Canada's position. Some other states, however, were reluctant to agree to such active involvement on the part of the Council, and they based this reluctance on the need to uphold state sovereignty. For the Chinese representative at the United Nations, this position would undermine the principle of state sovereignty.

Enforcement of International Humanitarian Law

The task of providing for strict compliance with international humanitarian law is one of the most important tasks today, primarily in connection with a great number of conflicts of different kinds. Strengthening of this law and ensuring its application are direly needed to ensure protection of civilians. Article 1 of the 1949 Geneva Conventions explicitly establishes that it is the states that are responsible for respecting and ensuring respect for international humanitarian law in all circumstances.(4) The pertinent provisions of the Geneva Conventions and the Additional Protocols should be observed in order to ensure respect for the neutrality of civilian populations. International humanitarian law has developed and has increasingly taken into consideration the need to stress the protection of the civilian population. With this development, various important standards, principles and norms have been set in universally recognized instruments to limit hostilities and protect civilian populations. Mention should be made of the Ottawa Convention on the Prohibition of the Use, Stockpiling, Production and Transfer of Anti-Personnel Mines and on Their Destruction for the protection of civilians. To implement these and other similar instruments, collective political will should be mustered.

Preventing the recruitment of children is as important as demobilization. Both goals require a long-term commitment to education and vocational training and meeting of psycho-social needs, as well as to reuniting children with their families. Education helps re-establish stability even in the midst of chaos, both for children and families.

In establishing 18 as a minimum age for participation in its peacekeeping operations, the United Nations has set a remarkable precedent. The UN has recommended that this policy serve as an example for military forces and police the world over. Until the minimum age of recruitment is universally set at 18, the reprehensible exploitation of children as soldiers will continue.

Vulnerable groups of society, such as the handicapped persons, elderly, women and children in particular, should be protected from the effects of sanctions. When designing sanctions, it is important to contemplate the effects those sanctions might have on children and on other vulnerable groups. In the interests of these groups, sanctions should not be imposed without immediate, obligatory and enforceable humanitarian exemptions, along with mechanisms for monitoring their impact on these groups. In states under economic sanctions, the inadequacy of current provisions has resulted in high rates of child malnutrition and in maternal and child mortality. There is a need to monitor the humanitarian impact of sanctions on children and to create more efficient exemption mechanisms is an important step towards protection of children and other vulnerable groups.

Impunity

The impunity of those who perpetrate war crimes against civilians, especially children and other vulnerable groups, must be stopped. The Geneva Conventions and their Additional Protocols are applicable only to states parties. The problem faced in conflicts today is that most of them involve groups that are not parties to the Geneva Conventions and their Additional Protocols. The setting of international norms and rules to ensure individual responsibility for atrocities committed in times of war and to ensure respect for fundamental human rights would be essential.

What has increased the vulnerability of civilians is the activity by warlords in weak or failed states. Motivated by financial gains, often through illicit trade in arms and weapons, warlords let loose their agents who terrorize and brutalize local residents. In doing so, these warlords are aided and abetted by outside private groups and arms dealers who benefit from the marketplace of conflict situations. The recent adoption of the Rome Statute of the International Criminal Court (ICC) is a step in the right direction. This Statute recognizes children's recruitment as members of armed forces, their rape and massacre and the targeting of their hospitals and schools for what they are, namely, atrocities.

Broadening of the Concept of Peace

The ultimate way to protect civilians in armed conflict would be to resolve and prevent the eruption of armed conflicts, for an ounce of prevention is worth a pound of cure. The basic causes of humanitarian crises should be addressed through economic and social development, democratization, maintenance of national stability, confidence-building measures and ethnic reconciliation. The magnitude of the problem of the protection of civilian population has shown that the concept of international peace and security as seen in 1945 has evolved to a considerable degree. This concept involves presently not only the military factor but also factors related to social justice, economic and social development, democratization and good governance. On 13 April 1998, the UN Secretary-General submitted a report to the Security Council on the causes of conflict and the promotion of peace and sustainable development in Africa. (5) Translation of ideas contained in the report into action would go a long way towards prevention of conflict.

Also pertinent to the frequency of internal conflicts is the extent of socio-economic development, the gap between the affluent North and the poor South. In order to decrease the number of such conflicts and to lower their intensity, assistance to the impoverished peoples of the South should be ensured. The elimination of poverty could be achieved through socio-economic development involving cooperation between the North and the South.

Institutional social and economic development, which would contribute to a greater respect for humanitarian law, could also be achieved through the integration of efforts of the UN general Assembly, the Economic and Social Council, the Security Council, the UN specialized agencies, and other international and regional organization in cooperation and coordination with the states concerned.

Depoliticization of Humanitarian Action

Some UN representatives, like the representative of China, are of the view that there is a tendency in international relations to politicize humanitarian issues and interfere in a country's internal affairs under the guise of humanitarianism. They believe that such a tendency complicates matters and intensifies the conflict. (6) Access by humanitarian assistance agencies to civilians in need or by civilian populations to needed international humanitarian assistance is of great importance. In a number of conflicts, humanitarian action has always been—or has recently become—impossible because parties to the conflict regarded humanitarian action as dictated by political considerations or interference in their internal affairs.

There have been many incidents in which people engaged in humanitarian action were injured or killed by combatants. Such attacks have prevented the humanitarian workers from carrying out their job. Worse still, the presence of organizations for humanitarian assistance is sometimes denied.

It is recognized that such assistance should be undertaken with the consent of the parties concerned. International law provides that those in need should be offered assistance and protection. Most atrocities against civilians in armed conflicts are committed in places outside the reach of the international community, thus there are no witnesses to the slaughter of civilians. The mere presence in the field of humanitarian workers, just to witness events, would be a major deterrent and would contribute to a far-reaching degree to the protection of civilians. In order to secure humanitarian access, political solutions need to be promoted while finding ways to reach civilians at risk.

Various sources have pointed out that in a number of cases humanitarian assistance has contributed to prolonging conflicts by subsidizing, directly or indirectly, deliberately or accidentally, the cost of waging war. Needless to say, humanitarian assistance must not be used to strengthen the incentive and capability of warring parties to perpetrate acts of violence, particularly against civilian populations.

Stopping the Flow of Arms

Arms, particularly small arms, are proliferating. The devastating impact of such proliferation on the safety of civilians is illustrated by the many armed conflicts that are raging in many areas. The development and proliferation of light weapons have made it easier for younger children to use them. It has meant more combatants, increased intensity of conflicts, more destruction, more casualties, and more expulsion and displacement of people. In order to lower the levels of suffering of civilians and humanitarian workers, the flow of arms, including anti-personnel landmines, to areas of chronic instability needs to be stopped.

Every year landmines kill or maim for life many elderly, children and women. Landmines can still and do kill and maim civilians long after the combatants have left the scene of conflict. The coming into force of the Ottawa Convention on Anti-Personnel Landmines would help decrease their use and destructive effect.

A more concerted international effort to combat illegal arms flows should be made in order to stop the fueling of more armed conflicts. However, definition of such terms as "actions," "threat," "international and regional peace" is by no means easy. Such terms lend themselves to various interpretations, in particular because the terms have political dimensions. When one enters the domain of politics, one is entering the domain of interpretation.

1.   United Nations, Security Council, S/PV. 3977, 12 February 1999.

2.   Ibid.

3.   Ibid.

4.   United Nations, Treaty Series: Treaties and International Agreements Registered or Filed and Recorded with the Secretariat of the United Nations. Volume 75, 1950, I. Nos. 970-973.

5.   United Nations, General Assembly, Fifty-Second Session, A/52/871 (S/1998/318), The Causes of Conflict and the Promotion of Durable Peace and Sustainable Development in Africa: Report of the Secretary-General.

6.   United Nations, Security Council, op. cit.

* The article was published in Dahesh Voice, Vol. 5, No. 4, Spring 2000.

My Brother, Don't Deny Me the Warmth of Humanity

My vocabulary is free from the restrictions of "I" and "they."
Humanity is my code of guidance.
Through humanity we are liberated from biases and intolerance.
My address is a home that stretches across the blue waters,
from the Caribbean to Hawaii, and from Tahiti to the Mediterranean.
My address is the earth with its beautiful colors and seasons.
There are no colors in my memory and humanity.
White for me is the color of snow,
of rice for the poor,
of glowing waves of sunshine for human warmth.
Black is the color of nature when it covers lovers with the warmth of privacy of love.
Compassion and love are the roads leading to my home.
God bless all peoples, all mankind.
With God's all-embracing mercy and guidance,
we are all the chosen creatures of God.
With love and humanity a rope of brotherhood and sisterhood unites my heart with all the miserable people on Earth.
The human creature born in Timbuktu I call him the brother from poverty-stricken Africa.
I swear to you, my brother, from far continents and different cultures, by the prophets in whom you and I believe, that I am looking for humanity to salvage us from the whims of ourselves.
It may be a source of joy for you, my misguided brother, to see all the evils in me.
Maybe this makes you feel you are superior.
You will not subdue humanity in me.
Let us learn the wisdom of the sages, who tell us the stories of man's miseries.
With my love, in support of humanity,
your heart will be cleansed from the evil ignorance of beautiful humanity;

it will free you from the bondage of bias;
and restore to you the immortal kingdom of humanity.
For my living and sustenance,
it is sufficient for me to fill the stomach with barley bread and olives.
I can survive on a half-empty stomach.
My stomach, lungs and soul I know to satiate with the fragrance of orange and
lemon and apple from the Holy Land.
My brother, do not burn, with your fire, the orchards,
so that all of us be sheltered under our mother's green love and protection.
Don't, my brother, harshly treat the oceans, for they, with their human experi-
ences,
tell the immortal story of humanity.
One person lost is one too many.
Let, then, humanity, with one concerted humble song, sing
in all corners of the small Earth.
With our vulnerabilities and weaknesses we are equal.
The dictionary of my mind is devoid of the unfamiliar word of superiority over
my neighbors in the other continents beyond the connecting seas.
I left a share of dates and dry bread for your empty stomach, my brother.
This is the only food I have to share with you.
I do not lie down to rest, over-stuffed with food much needed by the poor and
miserable of generous Earth.
I have conscience qualms over the over-consumed dwindling resources of our
over-milked mother Earth.
It is inhuman that you do not sense my humanity, brother.
You have no right to deny me the warm shelter of humanity.
The oil of Divinity has blessedly covered my Earth-colored skin.
My breath is permeated with the spirit of the immortal to which both you and I
belong.
Where are the angels of good who come forth to salvage humanity from the over-
whelming whim of unsatisfied desire?
Where are the knights of good tidings who remove the thorns from the one road
of humanity to a world free from myths of divided humanity?
A world where the clasped hands of the east and west form an elevated bridge
to humanity in its happy march to self-assurance and peace on Earth.

A Song for Peace in the Holy Land

May peace lighten our hearts, children of Abraham,
Children of Adam.
May peace prevail, where bloodshed has long reigned,
Hatred in the domain of oblivion.
May all the children of Adam and Eve,
Share the warmth of happiness and the moon-like tranquility of assurance,
Free from the shackles of anxiety and the repulse of fear,
Where the mind and the heart have become questing eyes,
To see justice for all the tired but yearning human brothers and sisters,
Where grandfathers and grandmothers, pregnant with stories of
    thorns and tortured tears,
Loudly declare to the grandson, with great determination,
    the brave humanizing story of peace,
Whose golden pages stretch from our mother earth to the watching heavens,
And whose enduring letters, like a true love story,
With penetrating rays of daring hope were written.
May peace be there, where tanks have become tractors,
And rifles have become stalks,
On which vine leaves grow,
With whose wine the triumph of peace we shall perpetually celebrate,
Where men no longer talk the language of war,
Where the battle whinnying of horses gives way,
    as wide as the earth,
To the kisses of love, and red rose-carrying palms.
Let the message conceived in the heart of the Holy Land,
Digested in the minds of men and women, with a fainting hope,
Stamped in the hearts of the fatherless, of the widows,
Be one of justice, of mutual love,
And human dignity for all the creatures of God,

With their different but beautiful colors of skin and eyes and hair.
Let that message, stronger than one million strong, and one thousand tanks,
And more enduring than gold and steel,
Let that powerful message shine on me and us and you.
Let that message, with its irresistible force,
With its glowing letters of the ink of history,
Reverberate now and forever more.
Let the ink of history,
With its myriad of outstretched arms,
As long as a journey of hope and wait of a lover,
And with its beseeching and appealing eyes,
Sow the seeds of barley, with whose fruit to drink the toast of peace,
And grow the young fig trees, vines and olives,
In each village and town and home,
With their green leaves announcing to all,
From east to west,
The onrush of the long-awaited spring of life.
Let that message, with its blessings, overwhelm each grain of sand,
On whose shores, swimmers have but the soothing waves of fear-free joy.
Let its spirit travel high, high, to the skies,
And to the stars, so that the earthly creatures bring the tidings to
    heaven that humanity on earth has prevailed,
And that we sure deserve the God's blessings.

The Naked Soul

The fine literary production is the result of a condition in which the soul is naked and hence natural; not hidden behind the social restrictions and artificial shackles; a condition of frankness, nature and simplicity; a condition of the soul asserting itself and its existence; a condition of the courage of the soul to expose itself naturally, without wearing the artificial social mantle that hides the soul from viewers and passers-by. It is a condition of emancipation of the soul and its psychological, emotional and intellectual outburst into its unlimited space, singing with the goddesses of singing, loving with the *houris* of the sea, grieving as the grief of the bereaved mother, engaging in a monologue, or dancing with the moon and the stars. It is a condition denoting a sense of freedom from shackles; removal of the mask from the face, mind and heart. It is the aversion of the soul to accept humiliation, insult, slavery, hypocrisy and ethical vacuum. It is the soul's purification from its disgrace, and its discarding the dress of social and political myth. To be naked is to deal with things directly.

When the soul is naked, it is very bold, has a very strong self-confidence; it is as strong as the storm, as beautiful as the woman, with its kingdom as protected as the protection of the queen, as solid as the Great Wall of China, with its word as influential as the penetrating fast-moving arrow; its flow is not obstructed by the barriers of restrictions, superstition and legends and the falsehood of the restrictive outdated traditions. It flows out with creation; it streams, bursts out, roams uncharted spaces, and enters spacious emotional and moral worlds. When the soul is naked, one thousand knights in armor will not be able to invade its space, to destroy its castle, to violate its sanctuary or to subdue its pride. While on the earth, their arrows go astray, while being naked sitting on the throne of the heights of space, with increasing highness and glory.

When being naked, the soul apportions its fine touches or strong impressions on all people and all things.

When the soul is naked, its brightness is strong; things are exposed when reflected over it; through its bright nakedness masks are exposed, and hypocrisy, fraud and artificiality are exposed. Through its bright nakedness, beauty and ugliness, nature and artificiality, sublimity and meanness, truth and falsehood are exposed.

When the soul is naked, belles-lettres are naked, strong and daring; and prose and verse are burst forth into boundless space. The poetic blossoming, the artistic and literary creation, and the ingenious intellectual production emanate from the naked soul.

Creative production is a manifestation of the ability to create. For this ability to create there should be the ability to be naked; creation flows from this.

Thus, the soul builds the beautiful and fascinating home where only virtue and sublimity dwell, and where there is no place for ugly things.

When naked, the soul is sensitive to what and who is around it, shows solidarity with humanity, and opposes brutality, helps the poor, the hungry and the deprived, resists political and social exploitation, criticizes unjust and despotic rule and supports the miserable, the wretched, the distressed, the unhappy and the displaced.

When naked, the soul is not tarnished with stain and opaqueness; it is pure as the purity of the mountain spring, and sweet as the sweetness of the lover's kiss, innocent as the innocence of babies, and glorious as the glory of the prophets. Nakedness is the dialogue between the hearts, the smelling of the fragrance of the garden's rose, kissing the mouth of the lover and feeling the warmth of the lover's eyes. To be naked is the courage to reject submission to the myths and legends in society and to eliminate the gloomy structures nested in the self.

The naked soul is asserted only through this condition, and its relation with others is realized only through this condition; its truth is revealed only through its being naked.

Nakedness and difference have similar aspects, as in difference there are freedom, outburst and non-conformity with what one does not want to conform with. In difference, there is boldness to express the different view, feeling, emotion and attitude. In difference there is the elimination of mental, cultural and political idols. With difference, one finds and fulfills oneself. Difference is a wall with which one protects one's naked soul, and protects one's freedom and moral existence. With difference, one purifies the deep corners of one's self from the stagnant piles of legends and myths, from the ills nested in the depths of the self. Difference is beauty; it is renewal; the palace with one hundred windows; it is the garden with its marvelous roses.

It is the scent with its fragrant aroma; it is the harvest with its variety. Difference is the converse of intellectual inertia and mental impenetrability.

The 50th Anniversary of the UN

What is the magnetic force of the United Nations environment that impels people, whether on the job or after retirement, to remain physically and emotionally close to the UN? In part it is the unique UN setting, which brings together people from differing cultural, social, religious and national backgrounds—people with their visions of human relations and of the well-being of humanity. In such a setting one experiences inter-cultural relations at first hand. Indeed, through the official and unofficial interaction of the UN setting I have come to feel and realize the unity of human needs, of human nature, and of the beauty of humanity in all its diversity. I have come to discover the fallacy of quite a few assumptions about inherent differences between peoples.

Thanks to its rich cultural diversity the UN can serve as a proving ground on which to test the validity of assumptions as to the best ways of achieving the UN's purposes and principles through interaction at the global level. It can serve also as a kind of workshop to prove or disprove some of the assumptions about the best means to achieve a better world through human communication.

In spite of the world's economic, military and political tribulations that have reverberated in the UN—or perhaps because of them—the UN remains the symbol of human aspirations to security, peace and well-being, the symbol of the unity of the human race.

In the last fifty years our world has changed in many fields almost beyond recognition. With an almost universal membership of 185 politically independent states drawn mainly from the countries of the Third World, the UN is devoting more and more attention to economic and developmental issues. If this trend continues, as I believe it will, it is bound to be reflected in a restructuring of the Organization itself.

Younger blood is being injected into the Secretariat. However, the UN which these new recruits are joining is not the UN that was founded on the ashes of the Second World War but a UN with increasing responsibilities in various fields all over the world.

Notwithstanding the criticism leveled against the UN, I feel that one of its most important achievements is that it has served as an international forum for states—in particular the big powers—to voice their positions, get to know one another's positions and, hence, make their actions less unpredictable. In a number of cases this has averted political and military crisis and confrontation.

Despite the diversity of cultural backgrounds of the UN staff and the nature of the UN as a political organization made up of independent states, I am impressed by the level of performance of the UN Secretariat and the achievements of the UN in various fields, such as international socio-economic development and the improvement of the status of women.

Our world is one of strife between good and evil, between the sublime and the ignoble, between humanity and inhumanity. With the benefit of our rich UN experience, I think that we can enhance the positive, good side of international relations.

Toward a Theory of Rise of Civilization*

One of the major yardsticks of the worthiness of the human being, society and state is the development of civilization. Civilization has been given various definitions. According to one definition, civilizations are advanced cultures. (1) Culture, according to one definition, "is all the modes of thought, behavior, and production that are handed down from one generation to the next by means of communicative interactions—that is, by speech, gestures, writing, and all other communication among humans—rather than by generic transmission or heredity." (2) According to another definition, civilization is "a progressive development of arts, sciences, statecraft and human aspirations and spirituality." According to this, there are degrees or stages of civilization. This is the definition adopted in this paper.

Advanced civilizations emerged in Mesopotamia, Egypt and Syria around 3000 B.C. or possibly even earlier, and were manifested in agriculture, irrigation, establishment of kingdoms and empires, religions, temples, government, use of metals, administration, ship building, trade, pyramids, mathematics, astronomy, law and codification of law, the calendar, canals, writing, production of paper, literature, art and others.

In the Middle Ages up to the 15th century, the Arabs and Muslims produced a great and remarkable civilization. Arab and non-Arab minds flourished in the cultural and civilization climate created by the Muslim States during the Middle Ages and many scholars and philosophers such as Al-Kndii, Ibn Hazm, Ibn Khalduun, Ibn Al-'Arabii, Ibn Rushd (Averroes), Al-Faaraabii, Ibn Siinaa (Avicenna), and others numbering in the thousands made original and insightful contributions to civilization in various fields of knowledge. This civilization had a lasting impact on the world, including Europe. It was a major factor in the European Renaissance, which served as the intellectual basis for the West as we know it today. A considerable number of scholars from various parts of the world were influenced in their theoretical formulations concerning matter and society by Arabic scholarly writings either in the original Arabic or by translations into such languages as Latin, Spanish, French, Italian and English. Indeed, until the 17th century, scientific books in Arabic served as textbooks in a number of European universities.

Through dynamic interaction, cultures and civilizations are enriched by one another. The extent of such interaction has depended on various factors, the more important of which are the duration and intensity of the interaction, the physical proximity of cultured and civilized peoples to one another, the mental and cultural capacity of people to absorb new cultures, and the political influence of civilized people on others. These factors interact with each other and they, in turn, interact with other variables such as the political and economic order of a given society or state.

The influence of one civilization over another has been a function of various factors, including the extent of intellectual freedom, the extent to which a civilization has been able to strike a balance between the material and spiritual exigencies of the human being, and the level of advancement of each of the cultures and civilizations at the time the contact between them took place.

No people can objectively claim monopoly over the creation of civilization. The creation of civilization is a function, or result, of climatic and social circumstances and conditions in the broadest sense, including political, economic, psychological, historical and legal.

Social scientists and philosophers have advanced their ideas about the rise and decline of civilizations, using psychology, religion, kinship relations, climate, race, identity of those in control of the means of production and others as tools in explaining human behavior and historical process.

In this paper, an explanation of the rise of civilization will be advanced in terms of the concept of the net result of the interaction of values in society, with some references to the developing countries. A human society means the existence of a group of humans living in a setting of social relations, surrounded by a limiting natural environment. In any human society, influence, drawn from various sources, is exercised by individuals and groups vis-à-vis other individuals and groups. Influence means to cause a person or persons to do something or to refrain from doing something. There are psychological, economic, emotional, mental and other sources of influence.

Individuals' and groups' values are related to norms. A norm is a specific rule of behavior. According to Robert Nisbet, norms are "the adjustments which human beings make to the surrounding environment. We may think of them as solutions to recurring problems or situations." (3). Kornblum wrote that, "Any given norm is supported by the idea that a particular behavior is correct and proper or incorrect and improper." (4). He viewed values as ideas that support or justify norms. (5) Another definition of value is that property of a thing because of which it is esteemed, desirable or useful, or the degree of this property possessed. (6) Values, which belong to the cultural, economic, psychological and political fields, differ in their significance for the state of human society. They fulfill human needs in social, psychological and biological domains. More socially significant and useful values are justice, freedom, democracy, preservation of privacy, primacy of the public interest, avoidance of hypocrisy, scholarship, emancipation of women, elimination of illiteracy, doing away with poverty, eradication of socio-economic and political disparity, achievement of peace and security, overcoming of inferiority complex, avoidance of the tendency to exaggeration, education, honesty, patriotism, respect for the ancestors and care for the cultural heritage.

Many of these values are institutionalized, in the form of habits, customs and traditions.

Values may have good or bad influences. The prevailing general ethical system of society—its prevailing cultural system, its conceived general welfare, its conscience and other elements—determines whether values have good or bad influences. Values may have good influences in some societies and bad influences in others; and vice versa.

Values with good and bad influences overlap, in the sense that a value can belong to two or more of the fields of values. For instance, education is a psychological, economic and social value.

There is interaction between values. In this interaction, values influence each other slowly or quickly, gradually or drastically, partially or fully, change, weaken or reinforce each other, conflict with each other, or are neutral in that regard.

Values are abstract or concretized concepts. It is the human being who is the agent of giving this abstraction concrete form. Human beings are the doers; they are those who give effect to the value. To have the value called "patriotism" concretized, there is a need for human agency to take some action, say, to salvage a nation from backwardness, which deserves the adjective "patriot."

Though values in their abstract and material forms exert influence on other values, it is the realized value whose influence is the greatest. Value influence may be conceived of as being extended on a continuum, starting from a value in its abstract form: the more we move on the continuum towards giving effect to the value the greater is that value's influence in society.

A mutual influence exists between and among influence-exerting value-oriented individuals and groups. These individuals and groups determine how, within the limiting natural environment, to make the values come into play in this dynamic interaction. Hence, such an interaction and its result are value-oriented. And the identity of people who wield major influence or power—the rulers or governors of the society at large, the people in control, the directors of society—is a result of the dynamic interaction of people with their various sources of influence and combinations of their values. Put differently, those who, as a result of this interaction, exercise a larger share of influence become the major influencers, that is, the rulers of society.

Human society is regulated at various levels in the various fields of life. This regulation is carried out, to a large extent, by the rulers of society. Shares of influence may be categorized as layers or levels of influence, starting from a minimum level and moving towards the highest level. The higher is the level of influence, the more general and significant is its effect at that level and lower levels. A ruling group that is committed to certain values, such as public responsibility and accountability, patriotism, learning or scholarship, would have more general and significant influence in giving effect to such values in society than that exercised by the commitment of one individual, a head of municipal council or a chief of tribe, an individual or a group wielding influence at a lower level. By the same token, the higher the level or source of influence exerted by people with values with bad influences, the greater the harm to society.

A society where, in the interaction between values with good and bad influences, values with good influences have a primacy over values with bad influences, and where influence at the highest level is exercised by people with values exerting good influences, would be a society where there is a greater likelihood for civilization to flourish, because it is there where justice, security and harmony are more likely to exist, which are some of the major foundations for the tendency towards innovation, creativity, and spiritual, intellectual and emotional emancipation.

Depending on the circumstances, development of human societies leads either to democratization or authoritarianism. In the Arab case, the Ottoman rule for four centuries and subsequent, and even consequent, Western rule were among the factors that disrupted the even development of Arab society and, thus, prevented the emergence of democratic regimes in Arab lands.

A minimum degree of intellectual and political freedom in society is needed for the flourishing of civilization. Absence of such freedom makes production of civilization more difficult because civilization is the product of innovation and members of society which lacks freedom are hardly innovative, as lack of freedom and the fear of the consequences of the exercise of freedom weaken the psychological motivation to innovation and creativity. Discouraged by the prevailing social and political system, innovation motivation disappears or lies dormant.

What has aggravated the situation in the developing countries is the heavy and constant economic dependence and want of the great majority of the masses in these countries. They are poor, ill-fed and ill-educated. Poverty is another factor which stifles the growth of civilization, as human beings must, necessarily, focus on mere survival before they can even contemplate contributing to civilization.

In some societies, there is a greater tendency to meet human needs through the actualization of values with good influences while, in other societies, the opposite occurs. In the former, there is a greater likelihood for civilization to flourish, because it is such values that are conducive to harmony, social assurance, self-confidence, social encouragement, social security, and dealing with issues in terms of the general interest—which, in turn, serves as a basis for emotional and intellectual emancipation.

The flourishing of any civilization requires a faculty that thinks properly, clearly, logically, rationally, objectively, disinterestedly and creatively. Civilization advancement involves innovation and creativity. In a society in which normative, in particular strict and rigid, conformism prevails, innovation and creativity are discouraged, restricted, opposed and/or met with indifference. Unfortunately, normative conformism has been very much in sight in many developing societies. This has weakened tendencies towards intellectual individuality and submerged personal individuality into the social intellectual collectivity or collective conformism.

It is important for the developing peoples to create and revive their place in civilization. Why is this important? First, the creation of civilization is taken as an indicator of human intelligence. In the present, as in times past, intelligence or lack thereof is an important measure by which peoples earn or do not earn respect. Thus, in order to be respected, society must demonstrate its intelligence.

Secondly, the human race is an agent of change in the social and physical environments. Civilization is a mechanism for causing this change.

Thirdly, the developing peoples are facing formidable challenges from outside in the security, cultural, economic and psychological fields at a time when they do not have a system effective enough to counter such pressures. There is probably no way to counter such challenges without the creation of a genuine and innovative civilization.

It is true that developing peoples have taken some steps on the road of development in such fields as literature, education, research, architecture, planning, organization and others. Yet they still need to travel a long way in order to bridge or narrow the gap between them and the developed countries with regards to many aspects of civilization.

The primacy of certain actualized values, such as a greater degree of intellectual freedom, of freedom from economic want, of a social and political climate which encourages innovation and genuine thinking, of education to promote independent and rational thinking and to seek practical ways to combat dangerous challenges, in conjunction with eliminating such behavior or institutions as authoritarianism, exaggeration, arrogance, marginalization of women, intellectual dichotomy and dependence on others, to name only a few, would be very conducive to the revival and creation of an advanced and universally respected civilization in the developing countries.

1. William Kornblum, Sociology in a Changing World (New York: Holt, Rinehart and Winston, 1988), p. 94.

2. Ibid., p. 85.

3. Robert A. Nisbet, The Social Bond (New York: Knopf, 1970), p. 225.

4. Kornblum, op. cit., p. 86.

5. Ibid.

6. (6)The American College Dictionary (New York: Random House, 1967), p. 1342.

* The article was published in The Arab American Dialogue, vol. 8, no. 4, May/June 1997.

Protection of Cultural Heritage as a Promoter of National Identity and Understanding among Peoples

Different cultures and civilizations are represented on the international scene. Cultural diversity is one of the most precious treasures granted to mankind. In spite of the passage of centuries, the heritage created by hundreds of generations has retained its value. As time passes it becomes clearer that the cultural heritage created by our ancestors cannot be dismissed as irrelevant to our present and future. Tangible and intangible cultural heritage is the accumulation of human experiences that humans have inherited from their fathers and ancestors who traveled along the path of culture and civilization, recording what they could produce, according to their thought and knowledge, whether through architecture, painting on walls, verses of poetry, by inscription on metal or leather, or by engraving on rocks, folklore, languages, oral and written local and national traditions and indigenous knowledge and other manifestations of cultural heritage. These traits were produced on all continents, and demonstrate the long path all peoples have traveled, with a long series of successes and failures

Cultural heritage is a common heritage of all mankind, regardless of its geographic location. This heritage is facing the threat of destruction because of wars and political extremism; it is exposed to dangers, such as the traditional elements of erosion over time and of changing socio-cultural factors that contribute to the deterioration or loss of this heritage. This has considerably damaged these cultural treasures in many countries. Today, over 30 World Heritage properties are considered "World Heritage in Danger." Many of these treasures are irreplaceable.

It is, therefore, important for the international community to work persistently together to make sure that we leave to future generations the treasures of the past by preserving and protecting this precious heritage which our forefathers have left for us. To achieve this goal is humanity's moral responsibility and obligation, owed to past, present and future generations. This goal could be achieved through global action based on the principles of international solidarity and cooperation articulated in international legal instruments aimed at protecting the world cultural heritage. Such instruments call upon the States parties to cooperate in the protection of the global cultural heritage. Acts that endanger cultural properties prove the need to reassert the spirit of such instruments. Such action has been taking place for years, and it is being coordinated and reinforced by a number of United Nations agencies, notable among them being the United Nations Educational, Scientific and Cultural Organization (UNESCO). Of these instruments is the Convention for the Protection of the World Cultural and Natural Heritage, which provides an ideal frame of reference for international legal instruments to protect humanity's cultural heritage, and because of the broad consensus it enjoys in the international community, having been ratified by some 170 States. This Convention is concerned with sites of universal value. Under the Convention, the parties recognize that the responsibility for ensuring the identification, protection, conservation, preservation and transmission of the cultural heritage belongs primarily to each state.

There are also the 1954 Hague Convention for the Protection of Cultural Property in the Event of Armed Conflict and its two Protocols, the 1970 UNESCO Convention on the Means of Prohibiting and Preventing the Illicit Import, Export and Transfer of Ownership of Cultural Property, and the 1995 Unidroit Convention on Stolen or Illegally Exported Cultural Objects, adopted by a special diplomatic conference held in Rome, fostering international solidarity and strengthening the measures defined in the 1970 UNESCO Convention.

Also, in 2001 the General Conference of UNESCO adopted during its thirty-first session the Universal Declaration on Cultural Diversity, which elevates cultural diversity to the rank of the "common heritage of humanity." The Declaration emphasizes that promoting mutual understanding and cooperation while respecting cultural diversity is essential for human development and for the attainment of peace. Cultural diversity is respected when one recognizes the others' cultures through the preservation of cultural heritage. Of much importance is also the Convention on the Protection of the Underwater Cultural Heritage, which was adopted by the thirty-first General Conference of UNESCO. This instrument aims to safeguard underwater archaeological treasures from the risk of market speculation, irretrievable loss and natural damage. The UNESCO General Conference also adopted a resolution inviting the Director-General to submit to the General Conference during its thirty-second session a preliminary draft international convention for the safeguarding of intangible cultural heritage. It also launched a new initiative against the deliberate destruction of cultural heritage. It is expected to have in the near future an international convention for the protection of the intangible cultural heritage.

These and other instruments have yielded significant results. One indication of such results is the emergence of the World Heritage list of 690 sites, of which 529 are cultural, 138 natural, and 23 mixed properties. They are located in 122 States.

In 1995, the World Commission on Culture and Development drafted a report, titled "Our Creative Diversity." The report, which was drafted under the chairmanship of Mr. Javier Perez de Cuellar, the former UN Secretary-General, is a reminder to the international community of the fragility and non-renewability of humanity's cultural heritage. This document, which urges States to pay particular attention to this heritage, drew a parallel between cultural and linguistic diversity, on the one hand, and biodiversity, on the other. It argued that cultural and linguistic heritage is necessary to preserve the reservoir of knowledge and intercultural communication, and that, as there is an endangered species in nature, there are also endangered species in the cultural world.

The proclamation of the UN Year for Cultural Heritage 2002 brought together representatives from all continents and a wide range of cultures and civilizations. The mission of Egypt took the lead in putting on the agenda of the General Assembly at its fifty-sixth session in 2001 the item on this proclamation and in preparing the relevant draft resolution. (A/56/L.13). This proclamation provides the international community an opportunity to further raise awareness to promote the importance of tangible and intangible cultural heritage, foster a spirit of peace, tolerance, mutual understanding and coexistence. This objective could be achieved through cooperation among intergovernmental organizations dealing with heritage, such as the International Center for the Study of the Preservation and Restoration of Cultural Property; non-governmental organizations, such as the International Council on Monuments and Sites; United Nations agencies, such as UNESCO; and regional organizations, such as the Organization of American States.

Protection and preservation of humanity's cultural heritage can also be promoted by organizing training courses, seminars and symposia. They can also be achieved by provision of technical and financial resources. Various countries, in particular developing countries, need such resources in managing their sites. Technology and expertise need to be transferred to local experts so that they can preserve their own cultural and natural heritage with a view to ensuring sustainable preservation.

Cultural heritage tells us a lot about connections, dialogue and mutual influences between cultures, civilizations and peoples. It can serve as a common ground for the promotion of mutual understanding and enrichment among cultures and civilizations. Cultural heritage—masterpieces of human thought in the widest meaning of the phrase—has for many centuries served peoples as an important source and background for maintaining their own identity, strength and spirit in the quest for development, well-being and prosperity.

Mankind's basic duty is to examione this heritage and to draw from its eternal values and lofty experiences, so that it becomes a legacy to our posterity along the road of development of human civilization. Through such an examination humans can discover their similarities, particularities and cultural uniqueness.

Through this examination, one people's commoin roots in the heritage of other peoples could be identified, and mankind's single source and single destiny of all peoples may be established.

While recognizing that cultural heritage sites are mankind's common property, each represents cultural property expressive of history, religion, traditions, philosophy, a particular way of life, a living knowledge at the heart of a community's identity, capacity for dialogue and interaction.

In this globalizing world in particular, where cultural particularities are weakened and threatened with being eliminated, people, in particular in the less developed world, are taking more interest in understanding and protecting their own cultural heritage as they endeavor to protect their cultural identity. Cultural heritage can serve as an essential source of cultural identity to each people.

References

"Charter on the Protection and management of Underwater Cultural Heritage, 1996.' Ratified by the 11th ICOMOS General Assembly, held in Sofia, Bulgaria, from 5-9 October 1996.

Gillon, J.K., "Cultural Heritage Charters and Standards." Gillonj.Tripod.com

UNESCO, Bureau of Public Information, "United Nations Year for Cultural Heritage: Priority on Reconciliation and Development." A Press Release no. 2002-18, April 3, 2002.

UNESCO. World Heritage Centre, Paris, France. The World Heritage List (2002).

Wise, Michael Z. "How Nations Wave the Flag of Culture." <u>The New York Times</u>, April 16, 2002.

The Territorial Significance of "Alladhii Baaraknaa Hawlahuu" According to Muslim Commentaries of the Qur'aan*

Allah the Most Exalted says in the first 'aayah (verse) of Suurat al-'Israa' (Night Journey) or Banii Israa'iil (Children of Israel): "Glory to [Allah] who did take His Servant for a Journey by night from the Sacred Mosque to the Farthest Mosque whose precincts We did bless, in order that We might show him some of Our signs: for He is the One Who heareth and seeth [all things]." (1)

Relying on various medieval and contemporary Muslim commentators of the Qur'aan, it will be shown in the following pages that by "Alladhii baaraknaa hawlahuu" ("the precincts whereof We have blessed" or "the neighborhood whereof We have blessed"), it is meant not only the immediate environ of Al-Masjid Al-Aqsaa (the Farthest Mosque), but also the lands that stretch far beyond its immediate environ.

Both Al-Maawardii Al-Basrii (d. 450 a.h.) and Al-Ansaarii Al-Qurtubii (d. 671 a.h.) have interpreted "Alladhii baaraknaa hawlahuu" to mean lands which stretch far beyond its immediate environ. (2) Both of these commentators stated that in that part of the verse, the blessings is with the fruits and river courses and with prophets and righteous people who have been buried around Al-Masjid Al-Aqsaa. (3)

Ibn Kathiir (d. 774 a.h.) wrote in his commentary on the Qur'aan that Allah's blessings are with the existence of "plantations and fruits." (4)

Hijaazii, after stating that Al-Masjid Al-Aqsaa is located in Al-Shaam, stated that the mosque's neighborhood is blessed with being a dwelling place for the prophets, and with the water, greenery, agriculture and stock farming. (5)

Al-Aluusii Al-Baghdaadii (1802-54) wrote that the blessing of Al-Masjid Al-Aqsaa's neighborhood is "with...its being a worshipping place for the prophets, peace be upon them, their direction to which they turn, and the abundance of rivers and trees around it." (6) He added that it is blessed with Allah's "having all the waters of the earth burst from beneath its Rock." (7)

There have been dwelling and burial places for the prophets and righteous people, fruit-bearing lands, water, greenery, agriculture and stock farming both in the immediate and non-immediate territorial environs of Al-Masjid Al-Aqsaa. Of course, there is no reason to understand that part of the verse as relating only to these places, fruit-bearing lands, water, stock farming, etc., situated in the imme-diate environ of Al-Msjid Al-Aqsaa.

As there have been no rivers in the immediate neighborhood of Al-Masjid Al-Aqsaa, then "the neighborhood whereof We have blessed," where river courses do exist, according to the Muslim commentators on the Qur'aan, must be located not in the immediate neighborhood of Msjid Al-Aqsaa.

Al-Maawardii Al-Basrii and Al-Ansaarii Al-Qurtubii stated also that Ma'aadh Bin Jabal narrated that Prophet Muhammad said that "Allah the Most Exalted says: O Shaam, of My land you are the choicest part, and to you I am dispatching the choicest part of My Servants." (8)

The term Shaam has included, throughout the Muslim history, Al-Quds Al-Shariif. Shaam means a northern region, the north, Syria. (9) According to Al-Mu'jam Al-Wasiit, Al-Shaam is the territory lying to the north-west of the Ara-bian Peninsula. (10) There is an Arabic expression which reads "shaaman waya-manan," which means northward and southward. To a person in Al-Hijaaz, Syria, including Palestine, which is lying to the north and north-west of Al-Hijaaz, is Al-Shaam.

Al-Maawardii Al-Basrii and Al-Ansaarii Al-Qurtubii cited this Prophetic Tra-dition (Hadiith) in the context of the interpretation of the Qur'aanic verse of "Alladhii baaraknaa hawlahuu." The fact of citing this Tradition in this context suggests that Al-Shaam in their understanding is the land which is a part of the blessed neighborhood of Al-Masjid Al-Aqsaa.

Al-Aluusii Al-Baghdaadii stated that in the Prophetic Tradition, Allah the Most Exalted "Has blessed between Al-'Ariish and the Euphrates and has endowed Palestine with holiness." (11) Again, the fact that this Tradition was cited in the context of the interpretation of the verse under consideration suggests that Al-Aluusii Al-Baghdaadii has understood the divinely blessed neighborhood of Al-Masjid Al-Aqsaa as stretching over all of Palestine, and further, namely, to the area lying between Egypt and Iraq.

It is very clear to Al-Haafidh Al-Suhaylii, as cited in a footnote in Ibn Kathiir's interpretation of the Qur'aan, what is meant by "the neighborhood whereof We have blessed." Al-Haafidh Al-Suhayli interpreted this part of the verse in a more explicit territorial term, encompassing the lands of Syria. Al-Suhaylii said that the meaning of what is lying around Al-Masjid Al-Aqsaa, which God has blessed, is Al-Shaam, that Al-Shaam in Syriac means goodness and that Al-Shaam was called with that name for its goodness and fertility. (12)

Al-Saabuunii, who is a contemporary commentator on the Qur'aan, also interprets "the neighborhood whereof We have blessed" as the land of Al-Shaam. He wrote that that part of the verse means "the neighborhood whereof Allah has blessed with sorts of sensory and spiritual blessings with the fruits and rivers with which Allah has endowed the land of Al-Shaam, and with its being the abode of the prophets and the descending place for the pure angels." (13) According to this commentary, the blessed neighborhood of Al-Masjid Al-Aqsaa is a part of Al-Shaam, as the fruits and rivers, with which God has blessed sensorily and spiritually Al-Masjid Al-Aqsaa's neighborhood, are those with which God has endowed the land of Al-Shaam.

1. The Holy Qur'an; Text, Translation and Commentary, by Abdullah Yusuf Ali (US: McGregor &Werner, 1946).

2. Abuu Al-Hasan 'Alii Bun Habiib Al-Maawardii Al-Basrii, Al-Nukat Wa-Al-'Uyuun (State of Kuwait: Ministry of Waqfs and Islamic Affairs, 1982), part II, p. 421; Abuu 'Abd-Allah Muhammad Bin Ahmad Al-Ansaarii Al-Qurtubii, Al-Jaami' Li-Ahkaam Al-Qur'aan, part X, p. 212.

3. Al-Maawardii Al-Ansaarii, op. cit.; Al-Ansaarii Al-Qurtubii, op. cit.

4. Al-Haafidh 'Imaad Al-Diin Abuu Al-Fidaa' Isma'iil Bin Kathiir Al-Dimashqii, Mukhtasar Tafsiir Ibn Kathiir (Beirut: Daar Al-Qur'aan Al-Kariim, 1402 a.h., 1981), 2nd vol., rev. 7th print, p. 354.

5. Muhammad Mahmuud Hijaazii, Al-Tafsiir Al-Waadih (Cairo: Matba'at Al-Istiqlaal Al-Kubraa, 1392 a.h., 1972), part xv, 5th print, p. 4.

6. Abuu Al-Fadl Shihaab Al-Diin Mahmuud Al-Aluusii Al-Baghdaadii, Ruuh Al-Ma'aanii Fii Tafsiir Al-Qur'aan Al-Adhiim Wa-Al-Sab' Al-Mathaanii (Beirut: Daar 'Ihyaa' Al-Turaath Al-'Arabii), part xv, p. 11.

7. Ibid.

8. Al-Maawardii Al-Basrii, op. cit.; Al-Ansaarii Al-Qurtubii, op. cit.

9. See, for example, Hans Wehr, <u>A Dictionary of Modern Written Arabic</u> (Ithaca, NY: Cornell University Press, 1966), p. 449.

10. Majma' Al-Lughah Al-'Arabiyyah, <u>Al-Mu'jam Al-Wasiit</u>(Cairo: Daar Al-Ma'aarif, 1972), part I, 2nd print, p. 469.

11. Al-Aluusii Al-Baghdaadii, <u>op. cit.</u>, p. 11.

12. See footnote in Ibn Kathiir, <u>op. cit.</u>, p. 354.

13. Muhammad 'Alii Al-Saabuunii, <u>Safwat Al-Tafaasiir</u> (Beirut: Daar Al-Qur'aan Al-Kariim, 1402 a.h., 1981), vol. II, rev., 4th print, p. 151.

* The paper was presented at the Twentieth Annual Conference of the Association of Muslim Social Scientists (AMSS), October 1991, at Royce Hotel, Detroit, MI. It was published in <u>The Arab American Dialogue</u>, vol. 12, no. 4, Spring 2001.

Structural Economic Imbalances Between the Countries of the North and the South*

Introduction

Economic analysts in the developing world are of the view that international economic relations should be based on global economic cooperation, economic interdependence and integration, on the grounds that this would contribute substantially to worldwide economic development and prosperity.

This view undoubtedly has its validity. The reality, however, is that the developed industrialized countries have not based their international economic relations on these concepts; rather, they have been guided to a great extent by what they perceive as their own economic interests without giving adequate consideration to the economic interests of the developing countries.

Developing countries have suffered from an acute economic crisis, reflected, in many cases, in economic recession and depression. It is grossly unjust to place the entire responsibility for the emergence of this crisis—as a considerable number of those who are interested in such issues in the West do—on the shoulders of the developing countries. This responsibility falls in fact on both the developing and the developed countries. This crisis is traceable to the political, social, economic and administrative circumstances prevailing in the developing countries, and also—and this is more important—to lack of an environment favorable for economic development, to lack of sufficient global economic cooperation, to the fact that developed countries have taken economic actions not inspired or guided by the two concepts of global economic interdependence and integration. This has militated against economic development. Developing countries are still laboring under this adverse environment, which thwarts efforts being made by the developing countries to achieve economic development.

This adverse international economic environment has manifested itself in—and has been perpetuated by—structural economic imbalances between the developed and developing countries. These imbalances—as this article will show—have made developing countries an arena in which developed countries have attempted to alleviate their own economic and financial pressures.

Elimination of such imbalances and the replacement of existing economic structures by new ones between the two groups of countries would significantly contribute to overcoming the economic crisis in the third world. How to bring about this change remains one of the major challenges facing mankind.

It is worth mentioning that developed countries have also encountered economic problems. These problems, however, have been much less acute than those suffered by the developing countries. What is more, the creation of new structures of economic relations would help to alleviate the economic problems of the developed countries.

In this article, certain economic arrangements will be proposed to help eliminate or reduce such imbalances.

Monopoly by a Few Countries of the Decision-Making Process

One such imbalance has been the fact that a very small number of Western countries monopolize, collectively or individually, economic and non-economic decision-making, with little attention to the concepts of global economic interdependence and integration. These concepts embody the principle of global participation in decisions on the world economic situation, and involve the necessity to accommodate the legitimate economic needs of both the developed and developing countries, not of the first group only.

This monopoly of decision-making has increasingly excluded the developing countries from the world economy. Needless to say, the industrialized countries have been guided in their decision-making by high political and strategic considerations to which they attach priority over other considerations such as interdependence, complementarity and cooperation in the world economy.

From the standpoint of world economic cooperation and interdependence and in view of the fact that countries of the South have been the more adversely affected by the current international economic order, it is up to the industrialized countries to accommodate, in their policies, the requirements of global cooperation and the need to create a global economic environment favorable for the development of all countries.

Lack of Financial Discipline Within the Developed Countries

Countries of the North, in pursuit of their domestic policies, especially in the service sector, have incurred considerable expenditure, with the result that they owe significant sums to various private financial institutions. These policies have not been helpful to the economies of the developing countries. The resulting internal financial pressures in the industrialized countries have found their reflection in the economic and financial policies pursued by them in the world arena. Their internal policies have been one important reason for national debt and high-level unemployment in both the industrialized and developing countries.

The developed countries, to cope with the situation, have taken economic and financial measures both at home and abroad. These include a degree of protectionism, considerable increase in the prices of exported products and considerable increase in interest rates on loans granted to developing countries. These measures have weighed heavily on their economies, increasing their foreign debts, destabilizing their financial markets and reducing the prices of their raw materials in international markets, consequently weakening any measure of influence developing countries might have on the world economy and international affairs.

Imbalances of Prices of Exported Commodities

What has greatly harmed the economies of the developing countries is the striking imbalance between prices of their basic raw-material exports and the industrial products imported by them. While prices of raw materials have declined, leveled out or slightly risen, prices of industrial imports have risen considerably.

A number of transnational corporations have greatly contributed to the decline in prices of raw materials. Such corporations, in pursuit of their financial interests, can largely determine the prices of third-world raw materials as a result of their control over major Western markets for such materials. At the same time, the exporting countries are vitally dependent on these export earnings. After all, the sources of developed countries' income are far more diversified.

The mounting foreign debt of the developing countries has greatly increased their balance-of-payments deficit and also the volume of resources flowing from South to North, aggravating the economic, financial and developmental problems of the South.

To contribute to the creation of a favorable world economic environment, a ratio needs to be established between the rise in price of industrial exports and the decline in price of raw materials and foodstuffs.

Protectionism

Developing countries, particularly small and economically vulnerable ones, increasingly depend on international trade to earn the financial resources needed in undertaking economic and social development and in shouldering the increasing burden of debts and debt servicing.

One of the structural imbalances has been the adoption by a number of developed countries of protectionism, intended to strengthen the domestic economy, but coming at the expense of other countries. This tendency has found its expression in increased customs tariffs and in quotas on imported commodities. The least developed countries, which have much less ability to achieve economic adjustment because of their weak economic and organizational structure, have suffered most from protectionism.

Protectionism has contributed to closure or dwindling of markets for developing countries' exports. This has caused a considerable decline in the prices of their exports. Competition among exporting countries themselves has ensued, making them decrease the prices of their commodities and enabling importing industrialized countries to control prices.

In 1988, the World Bank conducted a study which found that industrialized countries' protectionist policies had reduced the national income of the developing countries to nearly half of the volume of the official development assistance received from those industrialized countries. Consequently, abolition or curtailment of these policies would be essential to create the necessary conditions for achieving sustainable development in the developing countries. These protectionist measures and the resulting decline or fluctuation in the prices of the developing countries' commodities have contributed to the imbalance of the terms of trade, hindering their achievement of economic growth and development.

It is possible to do away with protectionism, or at least weaken it, through strengthening of the multilateral trade order and acceptance by all countries of the requirements of global interdependence and cooperation in the economic field.

Debts

For a variety of reasons, including those mentioned, developing countries have accumulated increasing amounts of foreign debt. This has engendered a world crisis with economic and political dimensions and has adversely affected development in the developing countries. One negative phenomenon has been the net transfer of resources from South to North; i.e., the sums transferred in the form of high prices of industrial imports and the cost of debt servicing in the countries of the South, have surpassed transfers in the form of meager financial aid offered by some Western countries.

With respect to the rising cost of debt servicing, it may be mentioned, for example, that, because of the considerable rise in interest rates, Nigeria's foreign indebtedness increased from 3.4 billion dollars in 1987 to 30.7 billion dollars in just one year. Cost of debt servicing has certainly been one factor in this increase.

The heavy burden of these debts has deprived the developing countries of the flexibility needed to adopt policies favorable for their growth and development.

To finance development in the developing countries, the huge volume of debts and debt servicing should be reduced, since it impedes the provision of funds needed for development. But this is up to the creditors, and until now it seems that the lending countries have lacked real will for such action. That is because these countries have been primarily concerned with their own perceived interests and have been beneficiaries from the economic situation prevailing in the world. The consequences of not helping would be more famine and deaths, and heightened migration and political disturbances.

* The article was published in <u>The Arab American Dialogue</u>, Vol. 8, No. 3, February 1997.

Arab-Americans: Some Reflections*

I am an Arab-American, and I am proud of it: the US is a great country of many opportunities, a country where law prevails, and whose constitutional system is predicated upon checks and balances. The Arabs are people with an ancient civilization and humanistic culture, and have made many contributions to world civilization. I with my wife have taken permanent residence in this country since 1969, when I came to pursue my doctoral studies. I have children and grandchildren who were born in the USA.

Compared to some other Arab-Americans, I may be regarded as a new-comer. Like other Americans, Arab-Americans vary in terms of the number of generations they have been citizens of the US. Some of them have been living on American soil for four, five or six generations (a generation is taken here to mean 20 years). US National Archives pertaining to immigration and naturalization certainly record that people from such lands as Lebanon, Syria and Palestine, which were a part of the Ottoman State, came to the US.

The number of Arabs in the US has increased, in particular in the last few decades. Arabs, both Christian and Muslim, reached the shores of the US from various parts of the Middle East, from Syria in the north to Egypt and the Sudan in the south, and from various countries of North Africa. All the Arab countries, in particular Syria, Lebanon, the Palestinian territories, Jordan and Iraq, namely, the Near East or South-West Asia, as well as Egypt, have been a source of this immigration. It is believed that Lebanese and Palestinian Christians were the first or among the first Arabs to immigrate to the US, in the late 19th and early 20th centuries. Some historical sources are of the view that Arabs set foot on US soil in the mid-19th century.

Historical, including American, sources indicate that ships carrying slaves from Africa, mainly West Africa, to America, both South and North, in the 16th and 17th centuries, carried not only pagans but also Muslims. Thus, it is erroneous to say that presence of Muslims and Arabs in the US is a new or recent phenomenon.

Old and new Arab immigrants reside in virtually all the United States, particularly Michigan, California, New York, New Jersey and Florida. Adults have come to the US either married or single. Adults and heads of households have different levels of education and a variety of professions, including medicine, academic teaching and blue-collar jobs. Hence, their incomes vary considerably. Their social and cultural outlooks are also different. Some are more liberal in their outlook; others are more conservative. Different levels of education and of incomes and various occupations are a major factor that determines their lifestyle.

When talking about foreign regions, including the Middle East, there is confusion among various sources, including mass media hosts and producers, spokespersons of social and national institutions and ordinary people, as to the geographical and ethnic designations concerned. A few clarifications are, I think, in order. Not all countries of the Middle East are Arab. Iran, Turkey and Pakistan are not Arab, though they are overwhelmingly Muslim. Also, not every Arab country is entirely Muslim, as there are many Arab countries, including Egypt, Syria, Jordan, Iraq, the West Bank and the Gaza Strip, where significant Christian minorities exist. Afghanistan, which many Americans know to be Muslim, is not Arab. Nor it is a Middle Eastern country, being situated in Central Asia.

Additionally, in a number of Arab countries there are ethnic minorities. In Iraq and Syria, there are Kurdish minorities. This is also true of non-Arab Turkey and Iran. In Israel proper, there are nearly a million Palestinian Arabs, Muslim, Christian and Druze, making up nearly 18 per cent of Israel's population.

Ethnically speaking, there is no such thing as a Middle Eastern-Arab. These lands were inhabited for thousands of years by their indigenous populations: the Canaanites, Phoenicians, Sumerians, Assyrians, Aramaeans. For many centuries before and after the advent of Islam in the early 7th century, tribes and groups from the Arabian Peninsula made the Fertile Crescent their permanent residence and mingled with the indigenous peoples. There are people with black, dark, brown and white skin, and with black, brown, blue and green eyes.

More than being ethnic, the term "Arab" is cultural. An Arab is one who is a descendant of an Arab or who speaks Arabic, has acquired Arab culture and who cherishes it. That is why under the umbrella of Arabness come people from South-West Asia, North, West and East Africa. Mauritanians, Djiboutians, and Sudanese living in the heart of Africa are Arabs as well as the Syrians and the Lebanese. Their countries are members of the League of Arab States, which has over 20 members.

Like the rest of Americans, Arab-Americans are neither more nor less faithful to America. For them, the 11 September attacks were tragic and heinous acts of terrorism. Perpetrators of such acts should be brought to justice.

Arab-Americans feel wronged when they are held guilty of this crime. They feel much pain; they feel they do not deserve this attitude from people whom they—the Arabs—appreciate and admire. Arab-Americans appeal to the sense of fairness of the American people. Arab-Americans love this country and they are willing to do their utmost to demonstrate this love.

There is a considerable degree of misperception by Americans of their Arab countrymen. Of the various reasons for this misperception, one is the less than adequate knowledge on the part of Americans of the affairs and character of Arab-Americans and of Arabs in general. All parties concerned, namely Arab-Americans, American 'experts' on Arab affairs, academia, the mass media and governmental institutions all share the blame for this inadequate knowledge. All actors concerned with disseminating a better American, and Western, knowledge of Arab-American affairs, attitudes and thinking should try to establish stronger and more intensive contacts between the American people and the Arab-Americans who, I know, regard themselves as an integral part of this country.

The arrival of Arabs in the United States, their living in it, their acquisition of US citizenship, and their experience of its social, political, economic and legal system were not a unique experience for America. As a virtually open society, a democratic system and an immigrant-absorbing country, America has become the new home of people from almost all parts of the globe. In this process, Arabs were not an exception. As people who came to this country under US laws with general applicability, Arab-Americans, it is fair to say, have a right to be judged with fairness by knowledgeable Americans and by the law of the land.

* The article was published in <u>The Arab American Dialogue</u>, Vol. 13, No. 4, Spring 2002.

Do the Arabs Deserve This Attitude?!*

Some Westerners like to lump the Arabs together into a single category. This over-simplification is due to ignorance, bias or to having a certain agenda. It does not reflect reality, and is based on inaccurate information. Lack of knowledge of a people—say, the Arabs—should not serve as a vehicle for demonizing a whole people as is happening now.

People like to say that the times we are living in are those of enlightenment and reason. I would like to ask how much enlightenment and reason there is when many in the West like to make unsubstantiated generalizations about the Arabs and attribute to them traits which, as humans, they lack, or which are found in all human beings. Many people in the West do not know that Arabs are people with an ancient, highly developed culture and civilization. They, as other peoples, have "good" and "bad" qualities. Is it too much for the Arabs to make this statement? Because of their humanistic heritage, Arabs probably have more humanistic values than those found in some parts of the West.

Like other groups, Arabs, whose presence in the United States dates back over six generations, have contributed to the culture and progress of this country. Their contributions in the fields of prose, poetry, art, scholarship, medicine, science and government are documented and significant. To name just a few, there are Dr. Michael Debakey, the cardiologist; John Sununu, Chef de Cabinet of the White House during a part of the George Bush Administration; Gibran Gibran, the poet and painter; Edward Said, who until his passing away served as Professor of Comparative Literature at Columbia University; and Dr. Ahmed Zuweil, Noble Prize laureate. There are literally thousands of others. These people were either born in the US or were born in various countries of the Arab world and then made America their home.

As a matter of fact, I personally and some other Arabs in this country take our less than envious situation with less bitterness, knowing that other cultural and ethnic groups have suffered, at various periods of American history and at different stages of their integration into the American society, from bias and ridicule. I do not feel that I need to cite examples of the ethnic and cultural minorities which are—to this very day—a target of this ridicule. It seems that the Arabs are passing through a similar stage. Certain external factors make their experience more difficult. The shorter this stage lasts, the faster the Arabs will become well integrated into the American society.

Human beings require certain attributes in order for them to qualify as belonging to humanity, including fairness and the need to approach fellow human beings in the spirit of human universality. How much of such requirements are met when other human beings, because of certain interests, are not approached with fairness and in the spirit of human universality?

Maybe the irony of the matter is also that our human psyche is split in this age of high technology, for when man stepped on the moon and when men are thinking about a human colony on it, some people are still giving ear and thought to such earthly matters as ethnocentrism, wedded to a wrong or imaginary idea about this or that people. Peoples have misunderstandings about each other, and this ethnocentrism makes such misunderstandings yet worse.

Maybe we can have an idea about such trivialities if we remember with awe that destiny dictated that we live in an incomprehensibly huge cosmos where some stars are separated from one another by a distance of many light years. And for those who are less than merciful toward the Arabs, they might not know that the people of the Middle East and North Africa are descendants of various peoples: Greeks, Romans, Crusaders, Jews Arabs, Berber, Egyptians, Assyrians, Canaanites, and others, and that the term "Arab" is a cultural concept, denoting a person with Arab culture.

I know, on the basis of my contact with Americans, that Arab-Americans have developed good relations with their neighbors in the United States. Does this situation not belie the negative image of the Arab in the minds of the people? Doesn't the fact that Princess Diana fell in love with an Arab, an Egyptian, send a positive message about Arabs? Does it not tell that he had such qualities that appealed to this late lady—may God rest her soul in peace—of the British royal family? Doesn't the fact that President Bill Clinton said, some time ago—and I am paraphrasing—that "if you have not met an Arab you have lost a lot," send a positive message about the Arab character?

The Arabs, who are on average less materialistic and more humanistic, are needed, I think, by the West. At a time of domination of excessive materialism, for the sake of a certain healthy balance in human psyche and society, it is good for this country and any country to have such a component of the population with a blend of materialistic and humanistic attributes that plays a more significant role in their attitudes and life.

* The article was published in <u>The Arab American Dialogue</u>, Vol. 10, No. 3, February/March 1999.

Arab-Americans and Teaching of Arabic in the US*

There are quite a few Arabic dialects. There are more Arabic dialects than Arab States which number twenty-two. In some states there is more than one dialect.

Arabic dialects have developed over a number of centuries. Different political, cultural and geographic circumstances in the Arab world have produced this multitude of dialects. A certain Arabic dialect is spoken either by the whole population of a state or by the population of one of its regions.

Dialects are mainly used for non-formal situations at work, at home, non-formal social occasions and interactions.

Besides the spoken dialects, nowadays there is the literary Arabic with its unified set of grammatical and syntactical rules. Called the Modern Standard Arabic (MSA), it is a formal Arabic which is spoken and written in the present-day Arab countries. MSA is the universal and recognized language of the Arab world. It is universal and recognized, maybe with a few exceptions, by the governmental and non-governmental institutions, the newspapers, literature, belles lettres, books in the physical and social sciences. Also, MSA is an oral vehicle of expression used in formal situations, including international gatherings and conferences, meetings of international and regional organizations, radio and TV newscasts.

MSA follows the same grammatical and syntactical rules as those of the classical Arabic, namely, the language of the Qur'aan, the Prophetic sayings, the prose and verse of pre-Islamic Arabia and of the rich classical Arabic literature and scientific contributions which were produced during the Abbasid dynasty whose seat was in Iraq, the Umayyad and other Muslim dynasties in Spain and Sicily, and the Fatimid dynasty in Egypt and Muslim dynasties in North Africa.

The major differences between the literary classical Arabic and the MSA are found in style and lexicon. MSA uses more familiar vocabulary and simpler style and linguistic structure. In it there are some Western, especially English, terms in use.

Arabic dialects are a blend of literary and distorted words in terms of spelling, pronunciation and structure. Social, cultural and historical circumstances have determined the extent of the closeness or remoteness of a dialect from the literary or the MSA.

MSA, rather than the dialects, is the language that is taught in elementary and high schools and in colleges and universities in the Arab world. MSA is the one that should be taught to Arab-American students in the elementary and high schools and in colleges and universities in the United States

The objective of Arabic teaching and learning in Arabic elementary and high schools and in schools where Arabic is taught in the United States should be to train the learner to read texts using MSA and to respond to it orally or in a written form. According to some estimates, acquisition by a student of an Arabic glossary ranging from 900 to 1300 words would serve as a good basis for him or her to know to communicate with others in day-to-day activities.

In formal social, political and economic circumstances, a few Arabic colloquial words and expressions are sometimes brought in MSA. When this happens it often happens when the warmth, relevance and expressiveness of the colloquial words are not escaping the attention of the speaker.

With the rising percentage of the literate and educated among Arabic-speaking people, the use of the MSA by the mass media, the greater exposure of educated Arabs to Arabic classical literature and their greater appreciation of their literary and scientific contributions in the Middle Ages, dialects are getting increasingly closer to the MSA which is penetrating more and more fields in the Arab life and institutions. Hence, one finds here and there in the colloquial language in all the Arab countries the use to varying degrees of literary words and expressions drawn from the classical and the MSA.

The distance is still considerable between the MSA and the dialects, especially in Algeria and Morocco, as a result of reasons, one of the more important of which is being subjected to strong French influence.

In view of this fact, it would be useful for the instructor in Arabic sometimes to make references, while reading an Arabic text, to a few colloquial expressions of relevance to the read text. Though there are many Arabic dialects, increased exposure to colloquial Arabic in the Arab world has made the Arabs understand some of each other's colloquial words. Of the various dialects, of the more widespread and understood ones are the Syrian, Egyptian and Palestinian.

A disputable question for a number of decades in the Arab world has been whether to accept or to reject introduction of Western, especially technical, terms to Arabic. Arab purists have claimed that Arabic has the terms which match the Western terms. Arab linguists have succeeded in locating some of these terms.

Over time there has been less opposition to accept Western technical terms, in particular those which have no Arabic equivalent.

In the pronunciation of words, besides using the letters of the Arabic alphabet, vowels (harakaat) are used. Diacritical marks are a feature of the Arabic script. They are the graphic symbols of the short vowels and other pronunciation features such as the sukuun, which is the vowellessness of a medial consonant. These symbols denote the kind of pronunciation of the short vowels and the sukuun. Such diacritical marks are used to control Arabic pronunciation. The Arabic text in the Arab world, with a few exceptions, does not use the diacritical marks. Such marks, however, are used in certain unclear cases, such as the use of the passive, of a foreign word, of verses from the Qur'aan or pieces written in the classical period. Arabs are used to read the text with no diacritical marks. Diacritical marks are used in the textbooks of the elementary and secondary schools in the Arab world.

For Arab-American students, diacritical marks are needed. Arab-American students, being unfamiliar with such a system, face a difficulty in understanding and using it. Use of such marks would make reading and understanding easier. To make this difficulty less acute, it may be advisable to have Arabic words in some cases transliterated. The Library of Congress has developed a transliteration system for Arabic. Other systems of transliteration have also been developed. It may be advisable to have less use of such marks at later stages of the learning process. This is a matter which the instructor can decide on the basis of his or her observation of the students' ability to read and understand the text without much reliance on the diacritical marks.

In Arabic there are many grammatical and syntactical rules. This makes learning of Arabic more time consuming and strenuous. And, after spending that long time trying to understand and memorize these rules, students would still have the feeling that more lessons need to be taken to improve their knowledge of Arabic. Because of the many grammatical and syntactical rules, and in order not to scare the beginners in the learning of the language, rules should be presented and taught piecemeal or progressively, with small doses.

In the teaching or learning process, texts need to be used. In the composition of texts, two approaches could be followed: a grammar-based approach, in which the text is built around certain grammatical structures, and a topic-based approach, in which the text is built around a topic. According to this approach, mention is made of the vocabulary and grammatical structures which the reading of the text of such topic requires, with due consideration, of course, to the beginning level of the student. With the topic-based approach of learning, the text can deal with social sciences, for instance, politics, society and culture. With this approach, students can reap a few benefits. An important feature of this approach is that comprehension is achieved through reading or hearing the language with a less attention paid to grammatical and syntactical rules. Centering on a common theme would help student better retain vocabulary and understand grammatical rules. A student would know the rules in the context of reading the text; a student does not learn rules in order to understand the text. Through the statement of a certain theme, words and sentences are related. Through this relatedness such rules become more manifest and meaningful to the student. With the adoption of this method, students are spared the scare or anxiety caused by the need to learn many rules.

In view of the little knowledge of Arabic gained by Arab-American students and of the above-mentioned merits associated with the topic-based approach, adoption of this approach is highly recommended.

Because of the apparent different levels of Arab-American students, the instructor should gear the presentation of the material to the students' levels. Instructors should avoid, as much as possible, going into complicated subjects in the language. They should present rules in as a simplified, easy and understand-able way as possible. They should refrain from going into subjects which are likely to cause confusion to the students. Presentation and explanation of compli-cated and confusing structures and topics should be postponed to later, more advanced stages.

As students may not be familiar with Arab pronunciation, instructors should speak at a slower pace and clearly.

Knowledge of Arabic by Arab-American students varies and it depends on fac-tors, one of them the extent of their exposure to Arabic during the early years of their life. Parents differ one from the other in terms of the attention they pay to their children's acquisition of Arabic. Children of new comers are more likely to have a better knowledge of Arabic than children of Arab families who have been residents of the UN for generations. Children of parents with a higher level of education are more likely to have a better knowledge of Arabic than children whose parents have a lower level of education.

Students' Arabic and English proficiency could be improved by making avail-able a classroom environment with a minimal stress. A stressful environment adversely affects students' self-confidence and their motivation to learn. Lack of self-confidence is a major factor for the limited Arabic proficiency. In order to keep students' self-confidence, instructor should also play the role of a conversant with the student, thus making the teacher-student relations less official and keeping them with fewer barriers.

Another factor responsible for the limited Arabic and English proficiency of a number of Arab-American students is inadequate professional preparation of some teachers. Some of them have no State-approved teaching certificates; others do not have adequate knowledge of the Arabic or the English language; others do not have adequate appreciation of the educational aspect involved in teaching. This inadequate professional preparation is reflected, among other things, in the unhealthy method of teaching which teachers pursue, focusing on instruction rather than learning, on overemphasis on the teaching of grammatical and syntactical rules rather than on the students understanding and learning of the text.

Languages differ one from the other in the extent of the semantic development of their vocabulary. An issue of relevance to the learning process of students in general is that of the extent of the semantic development of a word from material to immaterial meaning, and from a more concrete to a more abstract meaning. The English word "make" brings this issue into sharp focus. This word is more developed in English than other languages. Of its various meanings are "to manufacture," "to become," and "to be transformed." In many instances, Arab-American, and not only Arab-American, students use this word in the first sense, namely, "to manufacture," perhaps unaware of the existence of the other meanings of the word. Because of that, these students face a great deal of difficulty when trying to express in Arabic meanings of "make" in English in the sense of "become" and "be transformed." To relieve students from facing this difficulty, teachers need to explain this matter to students and provide them with the other translations of this word.

Arab-American students' Arabic and English proficiency could be raised by the use of Arabic and English in the class room. To realize their potential to to have adequate knowledge of Arabic and English speaking and writing, students need to be encouraged by the instructor to do that.

In order to make easier for Arab-American students to learn English, a number of features in the English language should be noted. As a language expresses contents in the two contexts of place and time, then it is of much importance to make students know to use the phrase of "there is" and its derivatives to denote existence. This phrase is much in use in several ways in Arabic.

What also slows down Arab and non-Arab American students' improvement of English proficiency is the difficulty they face in the understanding and, worse still, in the use of verbs and their derivatives whose meaning changes following the type of preposition which follows them. For example, the verb "give': give back, give birth, give chance to, give forth, give ground, give the floor, give in, give off, give over, give up, give way and more. In both British and American English there are quite a few cases like this. Students can understand and do understand the different meanings. But, it is much more difficult for them to use them. In order to make the learning process easier for foreign students it is advisable, at least in a number of cases, to teach verbs with only one preposition.

A problem which faces students in the Arab world and, perhaps to a lesser extent, in the United States has to do with pronunciation. Not every English vowel has a corresponding Arabic vowel. In contrast to Arabic, where there are three short vowels only, there are more vowels in English. Various English vowels which tend to be uttered in a certain setting of the muscles of the mouth, throat and tongue are improperly clustered or grouped into the three short Arabic vowels. Some English-Arabic dictionaries fail to include the transliteration of English words, thus providing Arab students with no help as to how to have a better pronunciation. This matter adversely affects the Arab students' English learning process as they, or some of them, face difficulty in having correct pronunciation, and might become self-conscious concerning their lack of adequate knowledge of English pronunciation.

* The article was published in <u>The Arab American Dialogue</u>, Vol. 13, No. 4, Spring 2002.

Technical Terms in Non-Western Languages, With a Particular Reference to Arabic*

To realize the aspirations of the peoples of the developing countries for cultural, political and economic development and to meet many of the challenges facing them in the scientific and technological fields, it is essential to develop a technological and scientific base for these countries. Development of such a base would require, among other things, that developing peoples acquire knowledge of modern skills in their own languages. Such knowledge would be helpful in keeping these peoples updated on new scientific and technological developments and in preparing them to make their own contributions in these fields.

For languages to be scientific, to be able to express scientific ideas, for serving as instruments for receiving sciences and technology and for contributing to them, accurate terms need to be produced and coined, that accurately express the meanings of corresponding foreign terms.

Arabic has been a scientific language for many centuries. The hundreds of thousands of scientific books and manuscripts that were produced by Arabs and Arabic-speaking Muslims evidence its scientific character during the Abbasid dynasty in Baghdad, the Muslim States in Spain and Sicily, the Fatimid dynasty whose seat was Cairo and other Muslim States in South-West Asia and North Africa. The eras of these states witnessed the peak of Arabic-Islamic scientific and civilization progress in the Medieval Ages.

Arabic has essential features which make it useful for science; it is rich in vocabulary; it accurately expresses meaning; it has a developed system of past, present and future tense; it has tools to distinguish gender and to express singular and plural; it has a system of inflection ('i'raab) which shows the function of the word in a sentence. It has demonstrative and relative pronouns, subject, object, predicate, active and passive forms, condition, substitution, nominative and jussive cases and many other mechanisms for precise expression of meaning. For four centuries in the Medieval Ages, it was the lingua franca of the world. During that time, books in various fields, such as mathematics, astronomy, medicine, optics, logic, music, geography, botany, geometry, algebra, chemistry, linguistics, history, philosophy and theology, were authored in Arabic.

The academies of the Arabic language in Cairo, Baghdad and Damascus and in other centers, such as the Center for Translation and Arabization in Al-Ribat, Morocco and, to a lesser extent, specialists in the Arabic language elsewhere, have produced and continue to produce many technical terms which convey meaning accurately in many fields. Not a few of such terms, however, have not gained acceptance and have been rejected either because they were not understood or because they were not to the taste of the users. Some of these terms were unfamiliar and others sounded strange. In many cases, academies for the Arabic language have produced different expressions for the same Western term. This, obviously, has not helped the standardization of the use of such terms.

Academies of the Arabic language and Arab linguists have made great contributions to the coinage of technical terms. Periodical magazines published by these academies contain serious linguistic research and new terms in the various fields. The academies of the Arabic language have added to the language of science tens of thousands of terms in various sciences and technology. Many Arab scholars, such as Butrus A-Bustani, Muhammad Sharaf and Anstas Al-Karmili, have left us a rich treasure of scientific terms.

As we are flooded with names of innovations of civilization and scientific discoveries in the chemical, physical, industrial and space laboratories, production of Arabic terms has not remained the sole responsibility of academies of language. This should also be the responsibility of individual scholars. As a matter of fact, creative individuals have made their contributions in this field. The history of the authorship of scientific terms in the era of Arab revival, which started in the early 19th century, attests to the useful role played by translators, literary figures, journalists and lexicographers. This history also attests to the many efforts made by language academies in establishing the guidelines for the formulation and translation of terms, in making studies about the principles of translation and in the promotion and publication of such studies.

In the Middle Ages, Arab scientific and translation institutions, such as the Dar Al-Hikma (House of Wisdom), translated and Arabized a great number of scientific and technical terms from Persian, Greek and other languages, and dictionaries in various fields were authored by a considerable number of lexicographers, including Al-Khalil, Ibn Durayd, Al-Jawhari, Ibn Mandhur and Fayruzabadi. Today, terms, such as qalansuwa, band, handasa, nafura, okianos, ustura and others, are regarded as Arabic and fit the Arab taste, in spite of their non-Arabic origins.

From the beginning of the era of modern Arab revival there have been those who believed that in Arabic sources there is a word corresponding to any foreign term in the sciences and civilization. Moreover, the Arab people and culture are being continuously flooded with new foreign technical terms. This flow has made it essential for Arab scientific and language institutions to coin Arabic terms or to find Arabic technical terms that were used for foreign technical terms in the Arabic books and manuscripts of the Middle Ages. Many made attempts in this direction. While some of these attempts were successful, there were terms for which Arabic terms were not found. Because of this and because of the continuing development and emergence of new technical terms, sustained efforts by individual Arab linguists and academies need to be made to coin technical terms.

The Academy of the Arabic Language in Cairo adopted a certain approach. This approach was reflected in a number of resolutions. One resolution provided that original words in the source language would be translated, whereas words with a universal naming and Greek- or Latin-derived words (such as telephone, telescope, microphone, microscope and television), words which are formulated in commemoration of a scientist or an inventor (such as Volt, Ampere and Watt) and internationally recognized words or letters (such as radar, laser, napalm) should be used in Arabic in their own form.

It would be a mistake to regard the form of any term as sanctified, thus excluding it from criticism and the possibility of change. Any linguist should be allowed to suggest a better word, in particular in connection with synonyms, which are still not widespread, or ones that lack in precision, thus making it difficult for it to convey the desired or intended meaning. Many of the synonyms coexisted whether with another Arabic synonym, such as "man's" and "taqa'ud," for pension, or with an Arabized term, such as "shurati" and "police," "hatif" and "telephone," "barq" and "telegraph," and "muharrik" and "motor."

The laws of "natural selection" and of "the survival of the fittest" work in the field of language through use, time and the development of the linguistic taste of people. Some words may seem unpopular, but they gain currency over time, and others may seem popular, but then they become obsolete. Words, such as "telephone," "telegraph," and "kerosene," which were rejected by many Arabs two or three decades ago, are being less opposed these days.

When translations derive from different sources, then differences in translations can be expected. A translation of a term, say from English, would not be in agreement with the translation of the same term from, say, French, when the

term does not contain a common Latin or Greek radical. Sometimes, two translated synonyms for one term seem as if they are unconnected because of the difference of the term's name in the source language: for example, "alluvial fan" in
English is "cone de dejection" in French. This difference is reflected in the Arabic
translation of the term from the two languages. English "nitrogen" and French
"azote," which have the same meaning, are translated differently in Arabic.

Arab linguists and academies of the Arabic language benefited from the flexibility that is provided by analogy and the derivative nature of Arabic. In many
cases, in the coinage of an Arabic word for a foreign technical term, the technical
meaning was completely lost. Examples abound: in the Arabic term, "darraja,"
the technical meaning of "two cycles" for "bicycle" is lost. "Hatif" does not convey the technical meaning of a phone from afar for "telephone." Moreover, compound Western terms were introduced by making a partial change in them.
"Television," for example, was partially changed into "telfaz" or "telefaz." With
this change, the term might sound Arabic phonetically or look Arabic morpho-
logically, but it involved sacrificing either partially or fully the technical meaning
of the compound structure of "television."

It is not possible to have all technical terms translated into Arabic. A reason for
this impossibility is that not all such terms have parallel expressions in Arabic. In
a considerable number of cases, Western technical terms were adopted without
change or with only a minor change in Arabic. This adoption might not please
Arabic language purists, but it helps standardize use of their forms. One of the
differences between Semitic and European languages is that in the former the
derivative feature is stronger than in the latter. Often, the structure of writings
and speech shows more use of this derivative feature in expressing meaning in
Arabic and shows more use of compound structure in expressing the meaning in
European languages.

This compound structure finds its expression in ways, including prefixes,
affixes and juxtaposition of words. The compound structure of European languages has given Arab linguists, when tying to express Western technical terms,
two alternatives: either to use the derivative mechanism or to use the compound
structure. Though they used both avenues, it seems that the second avenue is
being more resorted to, especially in the case of technical and physical terms. A
list of European prefixes and their often-used corresponding Arabic ones follows.

Bi-	thunaa'i
Circum-	hawla
De-	maani', muziil, mudhhib, naazi' or mubtil
Dis-	mufarriq, mukhtalif, naazi', naabidh, faasil, mufattit or musharrid
Hol- or holo-	kaamil, 'aamm, taamm or kull
Homo-	mutajaanis, mutamaathil or mutashaabih
Hyper-	mufrit or zaa'id
Hyps- or hypso-	murtafi'
In- or im-	'adam or ghayr
Iso-	mutasaawin or muta'aadil
Macr- or macro-	kabiir, 'adhiim or madiid
Mal-	mukhti' or naaqis
Meg- or mega-	kabiir or malyoon
Megal- or megalo-	dakhm
Mes- or meso-	wasat, mutawassit or maa bayna
Met- or meta-	maa waraa'a, fii maa waraa'a, mutahawwil or mutabaddil
Mis-	mukhti' or musii'
Ne- or neo-	muhdath or muwallad
Neur- or neuro-	'asabii
Omni-	'aamm or kull
Ortho-	mustaqiim, sahiih or 'aamuudii
Palae- or palaeo-	qadiim, 'atiiq or qabla al-taariikh
Peri-	muhiit or mutiif
Petr- or petro-	sakhr, hajar or naft
Photo-	daw'ii
Poly-	kathiir or muta'addid
Pre-	saabiq, qabla or muqaddaman
Prot- or proto-	awwalii or aslii

Pseudo-	mudda'a, zaa'if or kaadhib
Quadri-	ruba'ii
Tria-	muthallath or thulaathii
Uni-	uhaadii or wahiid

Selected Bibliography

Abboud, Peter F. (ed). 1983. *Elementary Modern Standard Arabic*. Cambridge: Cambridge University Press.

Al-Khatib, Ahmad Sh. (comp and ed). 1982. *A New Dictionary of Scientific and Technical Terms: English-*

Arabic with Illustrations. Fifth ed. Beirut: Librairie du Liban.

Oxford Illustrated Dictionary. 1965. London: Oxford University Press.

Speck, G. 1967. *A Compact Science Dictionary*. London: Pan Books.

United Nations. Department of Conference Services. Translation Division. Documentation and Terminology

Section. 1979. *Science and Technology for Development*. Arabic-Chinese-English-French-Russian-Spanish. ST/CS/SER.F/316. New York.

Guralnik, David B. (ed-in-chief). 1982. *Webster's New World Dictionary of the American Language*. Second

College ed. New York: Simon and Schuster.

Wehr, Hans. 1976. *A Dictionary of Modern Written Arabic*. Third ed by J. Milton Cowan. Ithaca, NY: Spoken

Language Services.

Wright, Sue Ellen and Wright, Leland (eds). 1993. *Scientific and Technical Translation*. (ATA Scholarly

Monograph Series VI). Amsterdam and Philadelphia: Benjamins.

* The paper was presented at the International Federation of Translator's XVI World Congress in Vancouver, B.C., Canada, August 7-10, 2002. The Congress addressed "Translation: New Ideas for a New Century." The paper was published in <u>The Arab American Dialogue</u>, Vol. 14, No. 2, Fall 2002.

Cultural Background and Choice of Vocabulary in Interpretation: The Case of Hebrew-English and Arabic-English Interpretation *

Introduction

Cultural background is a major factor in determining the style of expression. Social background, which is culturally conditioned, consequently is a factor in determining the choice of vocabulary used in linguistic expression. Hence, speakers from different cultures have different styles of such expression. This difference is reflected in the vocabulary used by interpreters (and this applies to translators). With the aim of improving interpretation and, hence, communication between speakers from two different cultures, an interpreter has an additional task to fulfill, namely, to choose those culturally conditioned expressions in the target language.

In this paper, treatment of the cultural influence on the choice of vocabulary in interpretation is conducted in the context of interpretation between English, on the one hand, and Hebrew and Arabic, on the other.

The paper sets as its aim to prove that cultural differences between English-speaking audiences and Arabic- and Hebrew-speaking audiences make linguistic expressions in the interpretation of the same speech different.

The method utilized in this paper is contextual and empirical. Interpretations between Arabic and English and Hebrew and English of speech involving the two pairs of languages at the United Nations in New York for the past 20 years serve as the text and context of study. The presenter's conclusions are based on his direct exposure to the interpretations of live and actual day-to-day speech between English-speaking and Hebrew- and Arabic-speaking people.

◆   ◆   ◆

An interpreter's cultural and linguistic background affects interpretation. The difficulty, and in some cases the impossibility, of accurate interpretation is in evidence in all languages, including that between Arabic and English and between Hebrew and English, and in all the linguistic and cultural contexts. One reason for this difficulty is that the style of writing or speech in a language has a cultural context that is peculiar to the social and cultural linguistic environment in which the speech is molded. (1) It is difficult or impossible for the interpreter to transmit precisely to the target language an expression with its cultural peculiarities of the people of the language of origin. This difficulty, however, is more in evidence with target languages whose peoples have not made considerable scientific progress. Thus, developing peoples always face the problem of the inadequacy of the translation of scientific, technological and cultural materials into their languages.

Culture is the way individuals deal with each other in social and natural settings. (2) The meaning of social concepts is a product of culture. Such meaning is a product of the historical, social, psychological, intellectual and economic background or setting of individuals and groups or of the background from which the concept has emanated. Such a background includes knowledge, experiences, intentions, circumstances, material and moral values and norms to the determination of which time and place contribute. These factors are the bases of such a background. A concept has more than one meaning, depending, among other things, on the differences of such a background. Meanings of a concept can be more specific aspects of a certain more abstract concept. For example, the more abstract concept of freedom means on a lesser abstract and more definite level economic, political and intellectual liberation, emancipation of women and slaves and freedom from fear and want. In a specific and actual setting of social relations each concept has a commonly accepted meaning. These meanings also contribute to determining a people's culture in a certain cultural setting.

If similar bases of a conceptual background are found for concepts—or meanings—this helps establish conceptual complementarity. This similarity establishes the connections among the meanings. Should concepts drawn from a certain socio-cultural background be used by people with a different background, a conceptual ambiguity is created, probably leading to conceptual confusion.

In different cultural and historical backgrounds a concept can have similar and different aspects at the same time. The extent of this similarity and difference is determined by the extent of difference or similarity between these backgrounds. Hence, from the perspective of the preservation of the cultural identity, it is wrong to confine treatment of a concept that has emanated from a different background to pointing out its aspects that are similar to the intended meaning, without stating its different aspects. Such a treatment would gloss over the different aspects of the concept that derive from the different background.

Some writings reflect a lack of awareness of the background of concepts. Western concepts that are accepted by a large number of writers in the Arab socio-cultural setting are separated from their Western background, and Arab concepts that are used by some writers in the West are separated from their Arab background. Such concepts are taken out of context and misused. To use in a target setting a foreign concept that lacks the socio-cultural background of that setting would introduce into that setting contents that are at variance with the meanings of the concepts prevalent in the target setting, whereas such meanings might be valued by the target audience. For example, the concept of the "survival of the fittest," which was articulated by some Western philosophers and has a certain currency in various parts of the world, is an ideological one that helps pave the way for domination. This does not mean that it might not be true. This concept is accepted by a considerable number of Arab writers. One would think that fewer writers would have accepted it had they known the ideological, historical, economic and cultural load of the concept. There is no absolute freedom in the Jewish and Muslim religious thought. According to this thought, God is the Sovereign over all creation and action. This is at variance with the concept of absolute freedom of the human being as conceived by some Western philosophers. To copy Western writings where the concept of absolute freedom is articulated, and to incorporate it into any other cultural setting where such concept of freedom does not exist are tantamount to forcing concepts into conceptual makeup of peoples.

The interpretation of "khalq," the Arabic word for "creation," is another example of the influence cultural, including religious, background exerts on the way terms are interpreted. As God, according to religious thinking, is the Creator of everything, then some Arabic interpreters, being influenced by this cultural background, use a word other than "creation" or its derivatives that convey the meaning of "creation," such as "to bring into being." This is the approach taken in interpreting this word even though the idea of "creation" in Arabic is expressed in such terms as "to bring into being." In spite of the same, or almost the same, meaning of these words, interpreters with religious awareness or sensitivity show more sensitivity regarding the use of the word "creation" and its derivatives.

Respect and/or reverence for holders of official or unofficial, governmental or non-governmental, authority traditionally and historically have a considerable say in the choice of Arabic words. One example is the word "yarfa'," the present tense of "raf'," meaning lifting, indicating or implying that the submitting actor or sender considers himself of lower status compared to the recipient. Thus, the Arabic word "to lift" is used to express the idea of submitting a report to a governmental authority; submitting a petition (in this case it is obvious that people submitting a petition have a sense of need for the people to whom the petition is addressed); filing a report or the like with an appropriate or competent authority; offering up sacrifices (in Christian traditions); initiating a legal action; or ascribing a Prophetic Tradition to an authority or a source. It also means to lodge a complaint against someone in, and to make an appeal to, a court. (3)

It is interesting to note that this use of the word "lift," "raise" or "offer" in Arabic is similar in one sense at least to that word in Hebrew. The Hebrew "he'ela," which means to raise, lift, bring up, cause to ascend, and its derivatives, also mean to offer sacrifice to God. (4)

Another example of the influence of cultural background on the choice of words in interpretation is the Arabic and Hebrew words for sovereignty. According to Islamic and Jewish theology, sovereignty over the world belongs to God. A religious Arab or Jewish interpreter would face a dilemma in interpreting sovereignty as such into Arabic or Hebrew. He or she is likely to try to find a word which is seen more acceptable as an interpretation of "sovereignty."

Again, by virtue of differences in cultural background, it would be unfitting, in some of the more traditional segments of the Arab and Israeli societies, to use the Arabic or Hebrew word for "shoes" in the idiomatic expression of "being in someone's shoes." (5) Instead, the expression would be interpreted as "to have another person's responsibility." There is no established use of such an expression in Hebrew in certain segments of the Israeli society.

Similarly, because of its feminine connotation, "skirt," in the idiomatic expression of "to hide under someone's skirt," in its Arabic interpretation would not be used. Rather, the expression would be interpreted as "to let someone else take the consequences of one's actions."

To regard the Western and Arab cultural-intellectual ways as unrelated opposites is erroneous and simplistic. That is because for many centuries, there has been a mutual cultural and intellectual influence and a considerable sharing of intellectual characteristics among the peoples of the Mediterranean basin. By virtue of this influence and commonality, whose effect is discernible until the present time, there has been some conceptual similarity in terms of universality of content among people of Judaic, Islamic and Christian faiths.

There are some differences in meanings of concepts in the Arab, Israeli and European societies. The meaning of freedom in a country such as Saudi Arabia, for example, is not the same as that in most, if not all, of the European countries. Strip-tease may be regarded as a free exercise in many parts of the West, but it is not regarded as such in many parts of the Muslim world, where it is regarded as dissoluteness. Yeshuv, which is the Hebrew for settlement, means much more than this in the Israeli thinking and recent Jewish history. It means the Jewish settlement in Palestine under the British mandate.

Although some Arab and Western concepts have a certain similarity, they are not synonymous or identical. Some writers in Arabic, when dealing with the issues of the Arab state and society, erroneously consider such concepts, as such as "shuura" (consultation), (6) as synonymous with Western concepts, thus attributing the Western meanings to the Arab concepts.

There is a relation between the nature of the concept and the ease with which it is adopted by society. The more technological the character of a concept, assuming all factors are constant, the easier is its adoption by recipient societies becomes and the less likely it is to be opposed to their cultural values. Given the more value-neutral character of technological concepts, there are fewer ethical and cultural prohibitions in society on the adoption of such concepts. By the same token, the stronger the cultural and historical character of a concept, again assuming the other factors are constant, the more difficult it is for other societies to adopt it and the more likely it is to raise questions within the adopting society about the extent of the harmony of the concept with that society's cultural and historical values. Hence, one of the factors that facilitate the acceptance of technological products in various parts of the world, including the developing countries, is their relatively reduced load of cultural and historical values.

Some errors take place in the interpretation between Arabic and European languages. A glaring example of this error is the use in Arabic of the word of "siyaasa" as an interpretation of the English words of "politics" and "policy." It is obvious that "politics" and "policy" have different and sometimes contradictory meanings. Some of the meanings of "politics" are the conduct of political affairs, crafty connections and factional scheming for power and status within a group. The meanings of "policy" include prudent or wise conduct, a course of action, plan or principle, as pursued by an individual, organization or government. (7)

This shows that the meanings of "politics" and "policy" are not only different from each other but that some of their meanings are also contradictory. Wisdom and sound judgment require consideration of the consequences of the conduct of matters, which does not go hand in hand with the use of cunning and unethical methods and recourse to the concoction of tricks and plots, which are covered by the word "politics."

Endnotes

1. Taysir Nashif, "Translation between Arabic and English: Points of Language and Style," The ATA Chronicle, Vol. XXIX, No. 5, May 2000.

2. About the meaning of culture, see William Kornblum, Sociology in a Changing World (New York: Holt, Rinehart and Winston, 1988), pp. 84-89.

3. Hans Wehr, A Dictionary of Modern Written Arabic (Ithaca, NY: Spoken Language Services, 1976), pp. 349-50.

4. Ehud Ben-Yehuda, ed. and David Weinstein, associate ed., Ben-Yehuda's Pocket, English-Hebrew, Hebrew-English Dictionary (New York: Pocket Books, 1964), p. 64.

5. N.E. Renton, Metaphorically Speaking: a Dictionary of 3,800 Picturesque Idiomatic Expressions (New York: Warner Books, 1992), p. 234.

6. See Al-Mu'jam Al-Wasiit (Cairo: Majma' Al-Lugha Al-'Arabiyya, 1972), p. 499.

7. See, for example, Webster's New World Dictionary of the American Language (New York: Simon & Schuster, 1982), pp. 1102-03.

* The paper is included in Proceedings of the XVII World Congress International Federation of Translators, Tampere, Finland, 4-7 August 2005. Ed. By Leena Salmi & Kaisa Koskinen (Paris, France: International Federation of Translators, 2005), pp. 116-117.

People and Their Priorities

It is necessary for the individual, group, people or state to set the priorities of their biological, economic, social and political goals and values. To set up a ladder or priorities would help ensure the survival of the entity concerned. Some goals and values are easy to discern that they deserve to be place at the top of the ladder of priority. Such goals and values include survival and the fulfillment of biological needs. The more a goal is connected to the fulfillment of biological and survival needs, the easier it becomes to determine that they deserve to be placed at the top of the ladder.

Individuals and groups experience different cultural, political and economic circumstances that are ever-changing, disparity in the speed of change notwithstanding. Such changes occur because of the continuing interaction among the individuals, and between them and social forces, and also between them and their natural environment. The place of goals on the ladder of priorities consequently changes. Yet, some fundamental goals, such as survival and self-defense, remain at the top of priorities.

For many decades, the Arab peoples have been controlled by local and foreign actors which restricted their political, intellectual and innovative freedom, and prevented them from exercising their will to self-fulfillment and improving their conditions. These actors have taken away much of their wealth, have contributed to preventing them from achieving progress and have sought to strip them of self-confidence by various psychological means.

From these circumstances a need has emerged to place on the ladder of priority, following achievement of survival, the dissemination and strengthening of the values of political freedom, democracy, independence, cultural awakening and revival, establishment and strengthening of the institutions of civil society, good financial and economic governance and building the personality of an Arab citizen who is proud of himself and of the lofty values to which he aspires.

Of relevance to determining the ladder of priorities is the form of government exercised in a country which is determined by the prevailing value system. This system is a product of the interaction of historical, political, economic and cultural factors on both the internal and external levels. Under a democratic system, there would be a greater degree of individual and collective consideration of priorities. In the case, however, of absolute rule, oligarchy, despotism or tyranny, the ruler himself usually determines priorities. Predictably, such has not been the objective determination of national or people's priorities.

Thus, given the lack of a democratic system of government in many developing countries, people's interests usually do not receive the attention they deserve; it is the ruler who sets priorities as he perceives them. In this he proceeds from the desire to keep his rule and from the considerations which the assumption and retention of power dictate.

In a democracy, people who assume power are more inclined to give priority to such goals as political participation, pluralism, equality, sense of citizenship, dissemination of learning and enlightenment among the people, provision of opportunity for citizens to express their opinions, and other democratic values. In a system of despotic or absolute rule, the ruler has often opposed people's awareness of the values of democracy and political participation.

In such circumstances, the ladder of priorities is distorted. For example, the balance is upset when tens of billions of dollars are squandered on the purchase of weapons while increased financial allocations for social and economic programs are not given a high priority.

The ladder of priorities, from the viewpoint of people's fundamental interests, is also upset when a large amount of time and energy is spent on the discussion of marginal issues, while less time and energy are spent on the discussion of fundamental issues such as the fate of peoples, coping with challenges which peoples are facing and identification of the sources of the peoples' weakness and strength.

Similarly, the priorities are distorted, from the viewpoint of the people's interests, when more attention is given to fighting minor evils than to combating serious evils, such as lack of freedom, lack of respect for human rights, stifling of the free word in its infancy, acceptance of humiliation at the national level, reliance on others in the fields of science and technology, inferiority complex vis-a-vis others, entrusting authority to those who do not deserve it, or being silent about injustice to which people are subjected, and the spread of corruption. When the ladder of priorities is distorted, fundamental goals, such as action for self-sufficiency in food, the goal of identifying the real enemy to the people, identification of the factors which weaken them and the endeavor to spread learning and combat disease are set aside.

Some goals, because of their urgency, occupy a higher place on the ladder than a goal which does not require immediate achievement and which bears delay.

There are various external factors which influence the ladder of goal priorities in a state. These factors include powers which wield influence over the state concerned, and the communications media, whose messages reach many parts of the earth. All states influence each other intellectually and behaviorally in the political, economic and artistic fields. States differ, however, one from the other in the extent of their influence on other states and of their being influenced by them. The extent of a state's influence on other states, and of its being influenced by them, depends largely on the state's economic, military, diplomatic and technological power vis-a-vis the other states.

A state which exercises influence is guided by its own interests and priorities. An influencing state which has set as its goal prevention of the spread of a certain idea on the international scene or in a certain region, for example, the idea of tribalism in the Arab world, seeks, in its relations with Arab states—relations in the economic, financial, diplomatic and military fields—to exert influence in order to make the governments of these states and various public and private organizations operating in them adopt a position supportive of the idea of tribalism.

Influence can be achieved through encouragement, direction, awakening of desire, intimidation, promise, threat, grant, deprivation or coercion in various fields. The method used depends on the priority which the influencing state attaches to a goal, and on the weakness or strength of the target state.

Peoples of the Third World are flooded with messages from the audio and visual media of foreign sources. The contents of these messages are controlled by groups which have their own economic and political values derived from their historical background and their economic, social and political situation. Their views do not necessarily coincide with the political, economic and social outlook of the Third World.

Messages from foreign communication media are transmitted to audiences in the Third World. A considerable portion of these audiences are influenced by the contents of these messages. This influence also has its say in determining the way Third-World peoples view their goal priorities.

This influence is not necessarily a source of pleasure and satisfaction as regards the interests of Third-World countries, because the messages of Western communication media do not originate in the historical, social, intellectual and cultural background of Third-World countries.

In determining the place of goals on people's ladder of priorities, the following considerations should be taken into account: the need to give high priority to the people's interests as a whole over the interests of smaller groups and individuals.

Goals such as achievement of economic, scientific, political and industrial progress for the people, administration of justice, democratization among people, provision of means with which to defend themselves, care for the weak or preservation of human rights should have priority.

Ethnic Affiliation and
Intellectual Objectivity*

Writers, whether they are researchers, thinkers or men of letters, deal with various issues in the fields of life. These writers belong to one country or to various countries, continents, cultures and civilizations. Often, discussions and debates are held among them in the desire to support an argument or to refute it or to demonstrate spots of weakness or strength in it. Nowadays, there are many vital questions on which Arab and Western writers agree or disagree—indeed, it seems that points of disagreement among them are more than the points of agreement. Politics, economics, history, culture, civilization, heritage, the past, the present, the future, progress, revival, modernity, the civilization role of the Arabs, impact of the social and political environment on development, the West's role in hindering or promoting development in the Third World, religion's role in mundane matters, Western cultural invasion or lack of it, the components of Arab personality and Western economic interests—all of these are questions which Arab and Western writers have treated. In such a treatment, intellectual agreement between Arab and Western writers has sometimes taken place, but in the great majority of cases, especially cases of alleged Western bias, cases concerning the foreign policies pursued by Western governments towards Arab states and other fundamental issues, the ideas of Arab and Western thinkers differ from each other and are often contradictory.

There are various methods to reach a scientific conclusion with a greater degree of objectivity. It is not possible to achieve full objectivity for a number of reasons, the more important of which is the impossibility to separate the self from the object. To reach such a conclusion, the researcher should take into account those methods, which include observation of the phenomenon under examination and attempting to be more objective and a greater separation of one's self from the object.

The extent of an idea or a conclusion being characterized by objectivity or accuracy depends not on the ethnic, civilization or continental affiliation of those who have done the study, but on the extent to which the student took into account the scientific methods which he should apply to reach a more objective and accurate conclusion.

Since the objectivity of a conclusion does not depend on ethnic, civilization or continental affiliation, it would be wrong to consider as objective or accurate a conclusion by a writer from a certain continent or civilization, a European writer for instance, merely because of that writer's being a European. Similarly, it would be wrong to regard conclusions by a writer affiliated with another civilization or continent, an Arab writer for example, as being subjective merely because of his being an Arab, or to attribute to a writer, from Uganda for instance, lack of objectivity merely because of his being from a country located in Sub-Saharan Africa.

This tendency to pass such a judgment seems to be a feature of a considerable number of Western writers. Many Arab and non-Arab writers outside the West have an impression—even a justifiable conviction based on writings in politics, sociology, economics and psychology in the West, the Arab lands and the rest of the Third World—that the percentage of Western writers who pass such judgment is higher than that of non-Western writers.

There are reasons for the wider spread of this phenomenon in the West, namely, the attribution of objectivity or lack of it according to a writer's ethnic, continental or civilization affiliation. One of these reasons is the belief by a number of Western writers that they have intellectual superiority over writers from non-Western countries. Another reason is the extent of a writer's knowledge of other peoples. It seems that non-Western writers have on average more knowledge of Western peoples than vice versa. It seems that some Western writers do not know how much flawed or shallow is their knowledge of non-Western peoples.

Arab thinkers, on the basis of their intellectual positions, have often set out to demonstrate the flaws in the thought of Western thinkers by alleging inadequacy, bias or selectivity. In doing so, they frequently quote—or invoke the conclusions of—Western thinkers whose intellectual positions are similar to those of Arab thinkers. In some cases, these writers were right in doing that, knowing that those Western thinkers pursued scientific methods in reaching their conclusions. In other cases, however, one feels that the Arab writer was not actually certain that such thinkers followed those methods, but rather believed that to cite a conclusion reached by a Western thinker would be more supportive than to cite a conclusion reached by a non-Western thinker.

It is not wrong, of course, to support a certain intellectual position, invoking conclusions by other thinkers, irrespective of their ethnic, continental or civilization affiliation as long as they have followed, in reaching that conclusion, the scientific methods. The intellectual history of mankind is replete with examples of invoking conclusions of others and citing their writings in support of a certain position. But, since that objectivity is not a function of ethnic, continental or civilization affiliation, it would be repugnant for writers to attach a greater degree of importance to writings of Western thinkers for the mere reason that they are Westerners. It would be objectionable from an objective viewpoint for writers enthusiastically to invoke a Western intellectual position in support of their position, merely because that thought is Western and its author is a Westerner. Whether it is fitting to invoke a certain intellectual position—be it European, African or Japanese—is determined not by ethnic, continental or civilization affiliation, but by the extent of objectivity and accuracy of that position. What might make writings of a Western thinker worth invoking is not the fact that the thinker is a Westerner, but the extent to which that thinker took into account the methods already mentioned, with a view to reaching more objective conclusions. Failure to observe this truth would be to accept the flawed view that Western thought is superior to non-Western thought.

* The article was published in <u>The Arab American Dialogue</u>, Vol. 9, No. 3, February-March 1998.

Perception of One's Own Prestige and Social Development, with Particular Reference to the Developing Countries*

The paper at hand sets as its goal to discuss the dynamic concept of the perception of one's own prestige. Examples will be drawn from the social realities of the developing countries involving the estrangement or contradiction between the requirements of the subjective and objective factors, thereby affecting the social setting.

In social activities, objective and subjective factors are blended in social concepts, such as stability, order, honor, dignity and satisfaction. An objective factor is one that the nature of the subject requires to be accommodated or taken into account. A subjective factor is one that is not organically related to the objective factor. Though it is impossible to fully separate the objective and the subjective factors, it is still possible, to a certain extent, to identify them. The lower is one's educational and intellectual level and the less developed is his sense of fairness, the more difficult it is, on average, to separate the subjective from the objective factors in one's own sense of prestige.

Perception of one's own prestige is based on objective factors, such as educational specialization, attendance of renowned colleges and universities, type of occupation, wealth, ownership of property and level of income, (1) and subjective factors, such as reverence for one who is or believed to be descendant from a family, respect for the elderly, class or place of birth, ascription of extraordinary actions to certain persons, and other cultural symbols. In some societies, affiliation with a particular religion or race is a source of prestige. The degree of prestige people attach to an occupation is heavily influenced by the education required for the job or the authority it offers its holder, as well as by income. (2)

Often, a contradiction arises between the requirements of the subjective and the objective factors. To overcome social underdevelopment, one has to give priority to the requirements of the objective factors over those of the subjective factors in his perception of one's own prestige. Not to do so would inhibit social advancement. But the individual tends to regard the giving of such a priority as an infringement on his sense of prestige.

It is assumed in this paper that the subjective factors override the objective factor of professional specialized occupation in one's behavior, contributing to the perpetuation of social underdevelopment.

Prestige is related to the exercise of influence. Sociologists and political scientists have made attempts to classify those who exercise influence. These may be seen in relation to some classification of structures of influence. One classification is that of wealth, power, status and prestige. Stratification systems rank people in more than one dimension. These four dimensions need to be considered in defining class. Remarking on the relation between 'class' and 'status,' Max Weber wrote, "with some oversimplification, one might…say that 'classes' are stratified according to their relations to the production and acquisition of goods; whereas 'status groups' are stratified according to the principles of their consumption of goods as represented by special 'styles of life'." (3)

Students of society differ regarding the degree of influence that prestige exerts. Gustave Le Bon wrote, "whether it be ideas or men, has in the main enforced its authority by means of that irresistible force expressed by the word 'prestige'…Prestige in reality is a sort of domination exercised on our mind by an individual, a work, or an idea…" (4) Le Bon remarked that prestige "…can be worn away…by being subjected to discussion…From the moment prestige is called in question it ceases to be prestige. The gods and men who have kept their prestige for long have never tolerated discussion. For the crowd to admire, it must be kept at a distance." (5)

Because of the intrinsic difference of perception, one's own perception of prestige differs from that of others. There are two types of prestige with both objective and subjective factors: a prestige that people ascribe to a certain person or view as enjoyed by a certain person; and perception of one's own prestige. In nearly all cases, however, some common ground exists; in other words, some subjective and objective factors of prestige are shared by both a person's own perception and others' perceptions of that prestige. In this paper, the focus is placed on the way one perceives his own prestige.

Lack of distinction, insufficient distinction or indifference to this distinction between the subjective and objective factors is one of the major reasons for the underdevelopment of science, culture and economy. For advance in these fields to be achieved, distinction between the objective and subjective factors needs to be made, and objective factors need to be accommodated in policy formulation and implementation.

A perception of one's own prestige is a source of gratification and a motivation to strive to retain such prestige for one who has this perception. Prestige also buttresses power and turns it into authority. John Adams has remarked that, "…The rewards…in this life are esteem and admiration of others—the punishments are neglect and contempt—nor may anyone imagine that these are not as real as the others. The desire of the esteem of others is as real as a want of nature as hunger—and the neglect and contempt of the world as severe a pain, as the gout or stone." (6)

Because prestige is a tool to generate and exercise social, economic and political influence, one who holds prestige attaches great importance to it. Because prestige is important in the acquisition of power, the exercise of influence and authority and psychological gratification, a person with prestige always tries to keep, protect and promote it. The higher is the prestige the greater is the likelihood of one's enjoyment of it and one's determination to protect and enhance it.

To achieve progress in the scientific, cultural, political and economic fields, it is necessary to recognize and take into account the objective factors in such concepts. Failure to do so is a major reason for the social—including political, cultural and economic—underdevelopment from which peoples—particularly in the developing countries—are suffering.

Development is a process of change which involves, but is not limited to, a greater degree of specialization, functional differentiation, experimentation, and more realistic and objective readings of situations. Objective factors in one's perception of one's own prestige are of relevance to the achievement of development.

Objective and subjective factors differ in the extent of their presence in, or proportion to, one's self-perception of prestige. This extent depends on such factors as the extent of one's educational level, one's professional and occupational level, one's upbringing regarding the values placed on democracy or on totalitarian and patriarchal systems, and the extent of one's respect for scientific approach.

In cases of contradiction, as usually happens, between the subjective and objective factors in the perception of one's own prestige, one has a tendency to accommodate the subjective factors and pays less attention to the objective factors. A person regards giving priority to the objective factors over the subjective factors as an encroachment on his prestige if his perception of his prestige depends on the subjective rather than the objective factors. This tendency is a main reason for this underdevelopment.

The following is an example of the contradiction between the subjective and objective factors drawn from the field of development. Social and economic development requires the availability of a considerable degree of people's participation in the process of development; this is unavoidable. However, one who holds the reins of authority—be he a governor, minister, mayor, chief of tribe, head of village, police officer, army commander or university president—may take, proceeding from his desire to keep his prestige, a hesitant, cautious, indifferent, reluctant or hostile stand towards the idea of popular participation. He may think, depending on his social and educational background, that such participation is inconsistent with the exercise of authority, which constitutes, in his own view and the views of others, one of the strong bases of his prestige. It is obvious that this stand would be a major reason for preventing or delaying development.

One factor for educational, scientific, economic and technological progress is knowledge, which is an instrument of control. It is obvious that taking account of subjective factors in one's perception of one's own prestige is not conducive to the acquisition of knowledge; rather, knowledge is acquired through taking account of the objective factors.

1.   Geraint Parry, <u>Political Elites</u> (New York: Praeger, 1969), p. 69.

2.   C.E. Rose and P.H. Rossi, "Gender and Jobs," <u>American Sociological Review</u> (June 1983), 48, pp. 316-30; P. Blau & O.D. Duncan, <u>The American Occupational Structure</u> (New York: Wiley, 1967).

3.   <u>From Max Weber: Essays in Sociology</u>, ed. H.H. Gerth and C. Wright Mills (New York: Oxford University Press, 1958), p. 193.

4.   Gustave Le Bon, <u>The Crowd, 1896</u> (London: Ernest Benn, 1952), pp. 129-30.

5.   <u>Ibid</u>., p. 140.

6.   John Adams, <u>Discourses on Davila</u> (Boston: Russell & Cutler, 1805), pp. 28-29, 40.

* The paper was presented at the 4th Annual Hawaii International Conference on Social Sciences, June 13-16, 2005, at the Waikiki Beach Marriott Resort and Spa, Honolulu.

Conceptual Orientation and Social Development

Among most thinkers there is what can be called 'dichotomous thinking.' According to this thinking, the conception of the existence of something negates the existence of its opposite. The conception of the existence of white, for example, is thought to negate the conception of the existence of black. This characteristic is manifested, in particular, in the conflict between the self and the subject of the thinking.

This dichotomous thinking reflects exclusivist and restrictive thinking in which the sweeping rejection or absolute acceptance of a certain concept or idea is manifested.

Dichotomous thinking proceeds as if there are no points or areas falling in between two opposite extreme points. As a matter of fact, mental conceptions can cover the whole gamut of the thing from one extreme to the other. Any color has many shades. In between the high and the low there are many points. Both height and depth have many degrees. This is also true of poverty and wealth, tolerance and intolerance, knowledge and ignorance and friendship and hostility.

Absolute Thinking is Dichotomous

Absolute thought is incompatible with intellectual pluralism and with relative thinking. In order for thought to be pluralistic, it must be relative. Absolute thinking is intellectual dichotomy. To ascribe a full attribute to something means a lack of sufficient knowledge of that thing. Between two absolute opposites, such as boundless beauty and boundless ugliness, and complete progress and complete backwardness, there are innumerable degrees or states falling somewere in between.

By the same token, it is erroneous to describe the experience of Arab modernization as a complete failure. Clearly, it is not a full success. In the same way, it is erroneous to say that all Western values have bad effects or that all of them have good effects, or that all Arab values have bad effects or that all have good effects.

As to the issue of intellectual dichotomy, it is erroneous to say that the many intellectual currents, such as liberalism, nationalism, capitalism, secularism, conservatism and sense of affiliation to one own country, fully exclude each other or fully accept each other. Some of these currents are similar to each other. These currents, for example, agree, in a general sense and without going into details, on such concepts as the need to preserve human existence and improve conditions of living. On the other hand, they do not agree on the concept of the egalitarian distribution of wealth.

Generalization can be an intellectual dichotomy. That is because generalization can be an intellectual opposite extreme, and thus a restricted and restrictive intellectual behavior. For instance, it is incorrect to say that European societies are fully advanced and that developing societies are fully backward. There is no such thing as full advancement or complete backwardness. Development is a continuing process that does not stop at a certain point. There is also dichotomy in saying that males are superior to females intellectually.

By the same token, it is erroneous to say that the deterioration of the Arab state is attributable to internal reasons only, to external reasons only, or to a single economic, historical, geographical, political, psychological, cultural or technological factor.

It is appropriate to avoid use of linguistic structures expressing intellectual dichotomy in cases where there is no need for such use. For example: only, unless, otherwise, "there is nothing on the surface of this planet except vile."

Similarly, it is appropriate to use expressions that do not encourage intellectual dichotomy, but rather indicate intellectual pluralism, open-mindedness, intellectual freedom and relativity. For example, "I might not be far from the truth if I said…".

An important means of weakening this tendency to dichotomy is to emphasize such factors as promotion of democracy, raising the level of living, promotion of the concept of "citizenship," achievement of security for citizens and last, but not least, raising the educational level.

These and other factors can be created gradually and in a synchronized and consecutive manner. But, in order to further weaken this tendency, it is very important for these factors to operate on a synchronized manner. The cultural, political, economic and psychological environment is much more capable of paralyzing the effect of each factor when the factors act in isolation rather than in a combined and synchronized manner.

The conception of the model of Western development and progress and of the model for any other region as contradictory is a conception that evinces dichotomous thinking. In any two models there are similar, if not identical, aspects as well as aspects that lack similarity. Marriage, happiness, law, order and many other concepts have similar aspects regardless of the model of development.

Obviously, human thinking has its problems. Two phenomena may be considered contradictory not because of an inherent contradiction between them but because of inadequacy of human understanding. A reason for this problem is the existence of cultural, intellectual, psychological and value barriers that prevent the delivery of the content of a phenomenon to the human mind.

Narrow Thinking and Open-mindedness

Open-mindedness weakens or almost eliminates the tendency toward narrow-minded thinking. Open-mindedness contradicts intellectual inertia and impenetrability, from which countries suffer. Intellectual habit is a reason for intellectual impenetrability. Intellectual inertia and impenetrability are present when individual behavior moves within the circle of limited and limiting intellectual conception and when thought in its relation to the surrounding social intellectual environment does not go beyond the known and familiar intellectual options.

Intellectual Interaction and Penetrability

In order for thought to be open it must interact with the social intellectual environment, and vice versa. If thought and mind are impenetrable they are not interactive. Interaction implies that one of the characteristics of thought proceeds from the assumption of incomplete human knowledge. This is the assumption that the working of the mind and what one knows are incomplete and inadequate, and that the increase of knowledge through interaction is psychologically satisfactory and scientifically and socially rewarding; and also that there is a psychological and intellectual willingness not to reject the new for the mere reason that it does not fall within our circle of knowledge and that it is new.

Philosophical, Logical and Rational Thought Weaken Narrow Thinking

What weakens narrow thinking is the greater use of scientific, rational, philosophical and logical reasoning. This could be achieved through making the learning of philosophy and logic part of the curriculum, and the learning of sciences and the promotion of rational thinking at an early age.

In some cultures there is aversion to, and bias against, dissemination of philosophical thought. The reasons for this attitude are ignorance and social conditioning. The latter implies going along with familiar matters and with some intellectual currents which think that teaching of philosophy might encroach on some intellectual and cultural orientations.

Undetached Thinking and Awareness of the Distance between the Individual and His Thinking

To foster understanding, it is necessary to create distance between the self, on the one hand, and the subject of thinking, on the other. Human perception tends not to make a clear-cut distinction between the self and the subject. Because of the organic link between the self and those subjects whose identity is determined by the self, not much distinction exists between the self and certain subjects. Scientific and philosophical thought helps considerably to create this distance, to strengthen it, to be conscious of it and to give consideration to it.

Ideological Affiliation and Partisan Thinking

Ideological affiliation creates partisan thinking, because that affiliation negates or excludes the domain in which that affiliation does not fall. The same is true of such phenomena as the domination of legends and myths. For thousands of years, there has been interaction between ideology and mythology. All people think with the aid of a group of values, principles, beliefs and assumptions, and with the aid of a group of legendary stories and biographies, folkloric stories and legends. Interaction takes place between the two groups. This mutual influence contributes considerably to the formation of ideology. The social context is an ideological and mythological context.

To generalize any ideological thinking leads to divisive thinking, because commitment to ideological thinking excludes other ideas that are at variance with the ideology. Given the fact that the ideological thought is narrower than the human reality, then to generalize any ideological thought is inevitably bound to be at the expense of the understanding of human reality.

Explanation and Divisive Thinking

It is mistake to explain social phenomena with one factor, neglecting other factors. Sigmund Freud perhaps tried to explain human behavior with one factor only, namely, the sexual drive, and Karl Marx claimed to explain human behavior by the economic factor.

Limiting explanation of social phenomena to only one factor leads to a dichotomy in thinking. This limitation excludes other factors in the explanation of such phenomena. It is wrong to limit explanation of the Arabs' political behavior to the nationalist, economic or religious factor or to the social or historical legacy only. It is also wrong to confine explanation of states' behavior to external or domestic factors only. Social phenomena have more than one factor to explain them.

Dichotomous Thinking and Development

Development, which involves change, can be gradual and smooth or forced. Smooth and gradual development is much easier to achieve in an intellectual environment where thought is conceived of as pluralistic and multi-shaded and not as stereotyped, intolerant and exclusivist.

As social development involves exploratory experimentation and a greater awareness of options, including options of thought and action, then the limited intellectual movement, because of the restrictive effect of moving within the known and familiar intellectual options, limits the range of options needed for development.

Development, which, as the word indicates, is gradual and progressive, entails, among other things, a greater degree of functional differentiation, of specialization and of rationalization. Intellectual interaction would make possible a smoother absorption, in the process of development, of these developmental features, showing a certain accommodation of, and certain sensitivity to, cultural characteristics in terms of attitude and behavior.

Besides its instrumentality in the achievement of development, logical, philosophical and scientific thinking contributes to development indirectly. This thinking, which is not intellectually restrictive, tends to weaken and perhaps eliminate restrictive and oppressive dogmatic thinking. More intellectual freedom and philosophical and scientific thinking increase awareness of the many dimensions of a phenomenon, of the multitude of options and alternatives of things, of the varying degrees of strength or weakness of a phenomenon. Being extremist and partisan, dogmatic thinking lacks this awareness.

Philosophical thinking, which can be hypothetical or unproven, goes beyond scientific thinking which must be verifiable. With its scope being wider than scientific thinking, philosophical thinking can provide more options and alternatives than scientific thinking, thus further weakening dogmatic thinking.

Because of its greater objectivity, philosophical and scientific thought helps create more distance between the self and the subject. This makes it easier to discover more intellectual options and alternatives, thus weakening dogmatic thinking and strengthening open-mindedness.

Slow Scientific Development in the Developing Countries

For centuries, human societies have suffered from the domination of one opinion in the political, cultural and social fields, and from the exclusion, rejection, harassment, or persecution of all others. Holder of a hegemonic opinion does not allow others with differing opinions to participate in an acceptable and legitimate way in society's life and intellectual interaction and creativity. He arbitrarily and falsely assigns negative attributes to those who hold different opinions. He might be a ruler, a tribal chief or a district governor.

The rejection or exclusion by the hegemonic opinion of other opinions is found, to varying degrees, in the entire world, but it would seem to be more prevalent and stronger in a number of developing countries.

The reasons for this phenomenon include a long history of political despotism, foreign oppressive rule and a patriarchal system, that cause the bold, innovative personality to fade away and promote blind intellectual imitation.

As a result, scientific development has been slowed down or prevented. Under such hegemony, a person is allowed to move intellectually only within the limits of that hegemonic opinion. Should he dissent from it, his life, family and finances may suffer. Out of fear of persecution, the holders of disagreeing opinions may prefer—except in a few cases of extraordinarily bold and altruistic people—to hide their opinions. Since scientific thought is invigorated by interactive thought, genuine and free intellectual interaction does not occur where self-expression is absent. In a condition of hegemonic opinion, the psychological and mental readiness to bring forth new ideas shrinks. People do not freely express their opinions when they anticipate that such expression will bring harm upon them.

In this prevailing environment of the hegemony of one opinion and the suppression of others, it is very difficult to promote and encourage philosophical thinking that by its nature is not necessarily tied to the prevailing thinking and intellectual structure. Philosophical thought, by its daring and unconventional spirit, can make a tremendous contribution to the achievement of scientific advance in various fields, to the promotion of civilization and to the discovery of social, natural and metaphysical principles and phenomena. Hegemonic opinion has not, to put it mildly, encouraged philosophical thinking, a fact that has contributed to the hindrance of scientific and civilization advance.

The hegemony of one opinion over others has a negative effect on scientific advance in another way. Because of this hegemony, a large number of thinkers—even some who have a tendency of independent thinking—have kept their written and verbal statements in line with, or not opposed to, the hegemonic opinion. With this development, intellectual freedom has been either further restricted or stifled. Since such opinions are highly likely to serve the interests of a small ruling group, whose thought is a reflection of its view of its self and of the world and is not, by virtue of its self-promotion, derived from an objective and comprehensive view, then such intellectual orthodoxy has come at the expense of the generation of scientific thinking.

Peoples would be able to achieve much faster and more significant scientific advance if they were to adopt critical thought that is dynamic and, hence, unending, as a means of better understanding and discovery and improving the conditions of their lives and societies. In developing societies, there are those who call for the adoption of one single cultural discourse. Such exclusivist adoption would remove any other discourse. To be confined to one intellectual school is inconsistent with the adoption of the critical intellectual approach. To be restricted or confined involves exclusion, whereas the critical intellectual approach is comprehensive, in the sense that it includes that which is confined and that which is not confined; it includes what is adopted and what is excluded by the one restrictive intellectual discourse. Because embracing one single intellectual discourse is restrictive, then it is intellectually flawed and narrow-minded.

Confinement to one discourse has another intellectual restriction from another perspective. Discourse is interpretative understanding. Restriction to one discourse means giving preference to one interpretative understanding over others, and it also means that one who calls for it falsely claims for himself a right to say that his interpretative understanding is more correct than others. It is more correct that the intellectual domain is vast and that every competent or qualified person in a certain context has the right to put forth his own interpretative understanding.

Politics has also adversely affected scientific advance in developing countries. Every person has different qualities, including those of politician and intellectual. As such qualities are in constant interaction, the human personality is complex. The difference between complex personalities, however, is reflected in the relative presence of each quality. Because of the difference between their personalities, their method of action and style of treating people and things differ from one another. The main quality that characterizes a career politician, for example, is dominance of his yearning to exercise a larger amount of influence and to assume governmental and non-governmental authority, while this yearning is less dominant among other persons. In the personality of the career politician, the component of care for personal matters is bigger than that component in the personality of the intellectual, in whose personality the tendency to criticize is larger than that component in the personality of the career politician. In the personality of the intellectual, the tendency to change or not to change for public considerations is more prevalent than it is in the personality of the career politician, whose willingness to oppress dissenters is greater than that of the intellectual, who may be more readily refrain from oppressing those whose views differ from his own and may have a wider margin of tolerance or a greater ability to turn a blind eye.

A career politician, because of his stronger incentive to exercise influence, has more influence in society and state than the intellectual. With that influence, the career politician can achieve objectives that the intellectual cannot. The intellectual sometimes has a need of the career politician, even though that intellectual may not accept the means by which a career politician has attained the ability to exercise the influence that may make him needed by the intellectual.

Because of the difference between the personalities of career politician and intellectual, and between their methods of action and style of dealing with people and handling things, the intellectual has a greater reason to reject the career politician's position and behavior than the latter has to reject those of the intellectual. Thus, their relations are strained.

In the developing countries—as, to varying degrees, in other countries—there is a group of intellectuals who enjoy genuine freedom of thinking, because intellectual freedom—and here I am talking about freedom as a relative concept, as there is no full freedom practically speaking—is associated with the emergence of certain economic, political, cultural and social structures that allow a degree of freedom of expression, without fear, of the critical independent view. Among these structures are civil society, an influential middle class, an established tradition of social and political democracy and the controls on official and unofficial political institutions. These structures are, to put it mildly, weak or absent in the developing countries. This weakness or absence has been a factor for the inadequate attention given to scientific endeavor, intellectual freedom and critical thought.

This condition has hampered the healthy development of society, because it is impossible for society to develop healthily without independence and freedom of thought and criticism, which are necessary to shed light on available alternatives of policy and action, and to make the possible conduct of genuine dialogue among views for the betterment of communication.

Many third world societies are still characterized by conservatism and are dominated by a blend of healthy and unhealthy traditions. These traditions and conservatism are reflected in patriarchal and undemocratic structures. These structures serve as a fertile ground for persons with official and unofficial political interests to stay in positions of authority. Given these conditions, and given the fact that objective, independent and critical thought inescapably aims at changing or altering these conditions, it is quite natural that those with such interests are fighting intellectual independence of political criticism and acting to marginalize and eliminate the role of independent and critical thinkers, thus hampering or slowing down scientific advancement.

Technological Education for Women as a Tool of Upward Social Mobility, With a Particular Reference to the Middle East

An Abstract

Education, including technological education, for women is widely recognized as a vehicle for upward social mobility. As pay tends to be higher for jobs in the technological field, technological education would lead to a higher percentage of women occupying higher-paying jobs, leading to enhanced social mobility.

Because of sexually differentiated role distribution, the roles of women tend to comprise a larger component of what are referred to in the paper as the roles of "reception, following and consumption," which suggest passivity. Technological education, which increases influence, would be bound to make women more active and involved members of society.

Influence is more associated with technological use, industrialization and urbanization. Thus, technological education and employment are bound to enhance women's mobility.

The interaction of science and technology with society will have a far-reaching say in determining the future of the peoples of the Middle East. Specifically, the study of science and technology is an important factor for the improvement of women's status in Arab society.

The focus of this paper is on the role of technological education in upward social mobility. Ways in which education brings about such mobility are addressed, followed by an attempt to point to the special effects of technological education.

Technological Education as a Vehicle of Upward Social Mobility

Education, including technological education, for women is widely recognized as a vehicle of social mobility (used here in the sense of upward mobility). Education would weaken the effects of factors that retard women's mobility. Technological education is more effective than general education in weakening the retarding effects of certain social institutions in the domain of social mobility. For example, it is more objective than education in the social sciences and humanities. Non-professional, extraneous factors such as friendships, nepotism, bribery and other factors may play a role in the choice of a person to fill a vacancy in technology. Thus, the one chosen may not be the most qualified to perform the job. In spite of that, with the increasing recognition of the importance of technology for development and given the greater spread of technological education and of social democratization in Arab society, with more weight given to professional considerations, the trend in hiring is one where women with such education will claim a significant share.

Education would likely to improve women's self-image. It would be a factor in discovering much of their potential. They would improve their understanding of the nature of politics, learn about their lives, society and state; they would become more aware of their rights, whether human, legal, economic, political or otherwise, and of the need to improve and expand them; and they would become more articulate in voicing their positions and grievances. Education would be likely to encourage them to engage in public and political affairs and to become more involved in matters that concern society as a whole. They would be more able to make their voice heard and taken account of.

Education would contribute to a better knowledge by women of their prejudices, stereotypes and other negative habits and customs that are a factor in their inferior conditions.

Education, Employment and Income

Discussion of the specific effect of technological education of women on their social mobility must take into consideration the prevailing social and cultural conditions and values, including the forces responsible for the subordinate position that women continue to occupy. At the present time, there are remarkable gender disparities in secondary-level and higher education in terms of overall enrollment. Women make up a smaller percentage of enrollment and the level of education of women is relatively low. There is a high percentage of illiteracy among women, the figure varying from country to country. The percentage of female holders of high-school and college degrees is much smaller than that of male holders of such degrees.

College education exhibits gender inequality not only in terms of overall enrollment but also in the nature of the fields of education. Whereas there is a much higher percentage of women students in traditionally female-dominated fields of education, the percentage is much lower in traditionally male-dominated fields, such as engineering, computer science and natural sciences. There may be a sort of alienation of women from science and technology. The majority of women in higher-education institutions are concentrated in the humanities and social sciences. In vocational schools, women tend to concentrate on "feminine" non-science-based occupations, such as the arts, teaching, sewing handicrafts and nursing.

Jobs in certain sectors of the economy go hand in hand with a higher level of education and with particular fields of education. The lower level or complete lack of women's education and their tendency to choose traditionally female-dominated fields of learning have contributed significantly to reduce job opportunities available to them in both the public and private sectors. These same reasons have also held back the number of qualified women in higher-paid technical jobs. As pay tends, in important sectors of the economy, to be higher for jobs in the technological field, this difference in the nature of fields of education has been a factor in women having lower incomes. Technological education would lead to a higher percentage of women occupying higher-paying jobs, with the attendant consequences of enhanced social status, security and mobility.

Technology, with its expanding application and constant development, is reducing the heavy reliance on manual labor. With the increase of technology-based employment, some manual workers are displaced. As more men than women, relatively and absolutely, have technological education and employment, in case of displacement they would be relatively less affected than women. For women to be less vulnerable to the shift from a labor-based to a technology-based economy, they need technological education.

Technological Education Weakens
Gender Differentiation Roles

Human society is sexually differentiated in a considerable number of fields. This differentiation is easy to recognize, for it is exhibited in the roles of men and women, in their self-perception and in the way they relate to the world. Some forms of sex-differentiation are alterable. A primary factor that contributes to disparities between males and females in the nature of fields of education and in the percentage of both gender groups in these fields at the college level in the Middle East (and this is true of the rest of the developing countries and, in varying degrees, even the whole world) is the social and cultural perceptions and expectations of role distribution and assignment to members of each gender. These perceptions and expectations, which have their reasons, are combinations of objective and subjective elements. One example is the social perception—perhaps enhanced by educational policies and practices—of women as biological reproducers and producers of a future workforce. This works in the direction of deepening the subordination of women and narrowing the range of functions they perform by influencing their ability to control their life opportunities at home and in society as a whole.

As women are biologically capable of adequately functioning in a number of fields that have been dominated by men, this role assignment reflects cultural prejudices, stereotypes and wrong attitudes towards them. Thus, women are channeled to fill jobs with lesser pay, contributing to their economic weakness and hampering their social mobility. This unhealthy state of affairs could be partially corrected by women's technological education, which would increase job opportunities with higher pay in the so-far male-dominated fields of education and employment.

Moreover, the structure of the college curriculum has a strong say in deciding students' performance. The curriculum feeds societal perceptions of women's roles in the family and society through gender-role stereotypes in textbooks. Social and cultural perceptions of the division of labor and expected gender roles leave their impact on patterns of gender disparity in educational processes and its results. (1)

Perceptions and expectations of role distribution and assignment have been an important factor in the concentration in certain fields of education and employment both for women and men, including paucity of women with technological education and profession. These role perceptions and expectations resulted in the emergence of a dependent-independent relation between members of the two sexes. This relation has its implication for a number of aspects of women's life and experience: attitudes, ambitions, mobility and others.

The 1979 Conference on Science and Technology for Development adopted a resolution on "Women, science and technology," which called on member states to facilitate:

"a) The equal distribution of the benefits of scientific and technological development and its applications to men and women in society;

b) The participation of women in the decision-making process related to science and technology, including planning and setting priorities for research and development and in the choice, acquisition, adaptation, innovation, and application of science and technology for development;

c) The equal access for women and men to scientific and technological training and to the respective professional careers."(2)

If the national objective is to bring about upward social mobility, then more women should be trained in non-traditional fields. In 1980, a UNESCO report on vocational and technical education for women arrived at a similar conclusion. The report said that men were accorded an automatic priority in educational planning, in particular in the third world. (3) Ways need to be found to encourage women to enter and perform well in non-traditional disciplines. This matter is recognized in the Platform for Action adopted at the United Nations Fourth World Conference on Women (Beijing 1995), which touched upon the need to improve women's access to vocational training, particularly in the fields of technology and science. The Platform further notes that women and girls are concentrated in a limited number of disciplines, and that governments should take action to ensure a better access by women to, and participation in, technology at the college level. Such action may include a supportive training environment and development of appropriate curricula and teaching materials. (4) To achieve this improvement, women should be provided by governmental and non-governmental agencies with information about the availability and benefits of technological education and of diversification of vocational training. (5)

Reception and Initiative

In various walks of life, including government, administration, teaching and technology, in all societies, and in particular third world countries, the roles of women tend to comprise a larger component of functions which could be described as reception, following and consumption (not necessarily in the material sense), whereas the roles of men tend to be those of involvement, in the sense of serving as a source of value producers, as pace setters, initiators and directors. This seems to be the dominant picture, even though sometimes intra-role and inter-role interactions take place across the social board.

Reception, following and consumption suggest, in a sense, passivity. To be passive in these fields suggests inadequacy of the ability to influence; it suggests that those playing such roles are the "objects" of the activities of those who play the role of the creators. In this state of affairs, when men are the dominant, the followed and the originators, and women are the passive followers, consumers and recipients, social mobility for women is very much affected. Thus, women can exercise little influence in promoting their interests.

Human society is a political society, in the sense that in every situation there is the use of influence to achieve certain objectives. In this context, men tend to be more influencer than influencee. With technological education, women's influence is bound to be enhanced as a higher percentage of women would be bound to be employed in the technological field. Women's role as mere recipients would thereby be weakened and their role as active, involved and influencing actors would be enhanced.

Because of its specialized nature, technological education has a considerable influence in shaping one's attitudes. It helps develop attitudes based on more distinct, differentiated and specialized concepts drawn from the domain of technology. This would be a factor that enables women to better articulate their ideas and positions professionally and socially, thus enabling them to be more effective in playing their many roles in the interrelated settings of the state, society, family and workplace.

Technological Education, Industrialization and Urbanization

The developing world has been witnessing a faster pace of urbanization and of use of technology. Industrialization and technological use seem, for several reasons, to coexist or to be associated with urbanization. Influence, be it economic, cultural or social, has been associated with such trends. Technological, more than non-technological, education is more relevant for such trends; it has more of a common ground with them; it is more instrumental in exercising influence. Technological education for women would thus be bound to make them more functional in the changing socio-economic system.

Technological Education and Entry to the *Public Domain*

Gender inequality occurs in various social "locations" or units of social organization, such as the community (public sphere) and the household (private or domestic sphere). For historical, social and cultural reasons, women are more associated with the "domestic" rather than the "public" sphere of social life. (6) This condition has a number of factors, one of the more important of which is the role of women as the mothers and nurturers of children. "Domestic," according to some sources, was defined as "those institutions and activities organized around one or more mothers and their children," and "public" as "those activities, institutions, and forms of association that link, rank, organize, or subsume particular mother-child groups."(7) This shows that the categories of domestic and public were seen as linked in a hierarchical relationship in which the public is more important than the domestic.

Jobs requiring technological education are more likely to be associated with the public domain. Thus, women's technological education and employment would mean their increased employment in the public sphere, where their voice would be better heard on matters of social, economic and political organization and management.

As technological education leads to technological employment, which helps employees move from the domestic to the public sphere, and thus enhance their influence, then women with this education would achieve a greater social mobility.

Merit for those with technological education is based on more objective criteria where achievement plays a more significant role. Because of that, in employment it is not subjective role perceptions and expectations which determine women's functionality and employability, but the objective element inherent in technological education. This would be an effective way to remove or weaken the effect of such role perceptions and expectations.

Patriarchal System and Its Effect
on Mobility

A patriarchal system has greatly contributed to the prevention of women's—and, though to a lesser extent, men's—mobility. The main features of patriarchy are control by the father of the behavior of children. This involves full authority of the father; the downward direction of instructions and commands, with no possibility of dialogue; and compliance by children. These privileges are ascribed to the father by virtue of tradition, where factors such as age, wisdom and masculinity make up a major component. In assigning to a family member only a role of recipient, follower and compliant implementer, the patriarchal system limits women's mobility.

Occupants of jobs that require technological education enjoy an important and recognized status independent of the patriarch's consent. As women achieve income growth, functionality as occupants of jobs that require technological education, and status promotion that comes with technological employment, without reference or relevance to the patriarchal rules, then the patriarchal system is weakened; it loses its grip on human mobility.

Notes

1. N. P. Stromquist, "Recent Developments in Women's Education: Closer to a Better Social Order?" In R. Gallin, M. Aronoff and A. Fergusson, eds., The Women and International Development Annual. Vol. 1 (Boulder, Colo.: Westview Press, 1989), p. 118.

2. United Nations, 1979 Conference on Science and Technology for Development, p. 43.

3. E. M. Byrne, Gender in Education (Avon, UK: Multi-Lingual Matters, 1990), p. 7.

4. United Nations, Beijing Declaration and Platform for Action Adopted by the Fourth World Conference on Women: Action for Equality, Development and Peace (Beijing: United Nations, September 1995), pp. 24-25.

5. Ibid., p. 26.

6. H. Moore, Feminism and Anthropology (Minneapolis: University of Minnesota Press, 1988); Michelle Z. Rosaldo, "Woman, Culture and Society: A Theoretical Overview." In M. Rosaldo and L. Lamphere, eds., Woman, Culture and Society (Stanford: Stanford University Press, 1974).

7. Ibid., p. 23.

Shared Basic Principles and Thought in Arab Society*

Dialogue is exchange of opinions in which one each of those engaged in it tries to prove the correctness of his (and this applies to the feminine gender) ideas and the fallacy of the other party or parties or of an audience on an issue, with a view to persuade the other party to bring his conduct into line. Dialogue means expression of thought without a great deal of restrictions. An important objective of dialogue is to attain a common area of agreement or common denominators. Dialogue in the Arab region—as in other regions of the world—suffers from a crisis. This crisis is a reflection of the political, economic and social crisis from which the inhabitants of this region suffer. In societies, like Arab society, in which considerations and needs of government assume priority over other considerations and needs, it is unavoidable that this restricts expression of thought, putting intellectual dialogue into a crisis.

Dialogue in the Arab region, as in other regions, also suffers from a social crisis. Any dialogue has a social, including political, economic, cultural, religious and methodological theme; or a theme related to a principle, value, idea or belief. An individual, brought up in any culture and place, has cultural stereotypes, partiality and emotions. It would be ignorance or self-delusion to think otherwise. This social, cultural and psychological makeup has various and varying degrees of impeding one's intellectual communication and comprehension of a theme. Communication is also more difficult because of the difference in lexical meanings, in one's understanding of them, in the extent of his understanding of events and developments, and in his interpretation of them, depending on his socio-cultural background.

In Arab society, social—including cultural, economic and political—currents vary considerably and clash with each other for a multitude of reasons, but especially because this society is passing through a transitional stage of social, political and economic underdevelopment on the way to development. It is but natural that this contradiction creates pressure and imposes a heavy restriction on the free expression of ideas. Given the fact that each of these currents tries to dominate the others, and that Arab society presently lacks well-established traditions of intellectual dialogue, then these attempts impair the possibility of developing and strengthening dialogue.

What makes engagement in dialogue more difficult is the insufficiency of human knowledge. Humans, with their history, legacy, needs and aspirations, are very complex. Many social and psychological phenomena are still inadequately understood. Science has its limitations in research into such phenomena. Accordingly, it is unreasonable and unrealistic and not in the spirit of humanity and scientific humility to claim that an individual, a group or a state is able to know all the answers to the questions of existence and to explain social and psychological realities, including needs and motives. Given the complexity of the human reality and the inadequacy of human knowledge, then ideas, explanations of the social and political phenomena, and policy premises are likely to be wrong. Hence, the categorical conviction of the accuracy of an idea or an explanation, the sweeping generalization about a culture or people, and the rushing to embrace certain ideas, leaving no margin for error—all indicate a defective grasp of reality, ignorance of the comprehensiveness and integrity of phenomena, indifference to the complexity of social and psychological questions, and lack of intellectual balance and of seriousness in treatment of issues.

What also makes engagement in dialogue more difficult is the difficulty of separation between the objective and subjective components of the human being. These components are constantly changing. An indication of the intellectual and emotional maturity of one is the ability to establish a certain distance between these components. With this ability he would be more able to gain a greater insight into issues with a greater degree of impartiality and objectivity, and to achieve a better intellectual communication, thus enhancing understanding of the others' ideas and experiences. Because of the attitudinal and behavioral effects of cultural background, it is impossible, whether in the developing or the developed countries, to have a full separation between one's cultural-psychological makeup and the object. There is a greater share of objectivity in the intellectual component and a greater share of subjectivity in the psychological-cultural-subjective component. One's understanding and definition of the object are a reflection of one's self. Hence, it is unavoidable that dialogue be influenced by that makeup. In order to make communication and dialogue more effective, it is necessary to establish a certain distance between the intellectual component and the non-intellectual component.

There is another reason for the need, when attempting to achieve communication and to engage in dialogue, to distinguish clearly between the intellectual component and the non-intellectual component of the human being. Because thinking is less subjective than the non-intellectual component, those attempting to engage in dialogue travel a longer road in intellectual formulation and exchange, while their subjective component would not have traveled that far. This lag is because the intellectual component is more easily satisfied with intellectual exchange, which is the cornerstone of dialogue, whereas it is much more difficult to satisfy and express the subjective component, which is seated deeper in the self, through intellectual channels.

It is not possible to achieve a meaningful dialogue without the existence of one basic intellectual point of reference. A point of reference is an accepted group of basic and general principles. Without the existence of such point of reference, expressed ideas are likely to be disjoined from each other, and intellectual compartments and pockets would be highly likely to emerge which would be independent of each other. In the Arab society, it probably has not been agreed on one basic intellectual point of reference. This has been a major reason for the crisis in the Arab dialogue.

Common denominators should exist in Arab society, but such denominators have not been uncovered. That is yet another reason for the crisis of dialogue. Also, the non-achievement of dialogue is a reason for the fact that such denominators have not been uncovered and that agreement on them has not been achieved.

To reach a common point of reference it would be necessary to strengthen and continue dialogue, because through dialogue it would be possible to uncover the common intellectual denominators which may constitute a point of reference. Lower intellectual level is one of the reasons for not uncovering such denominators, but the more important factor is the political factor. What is meant by the political factor is the existence of governmental and non-governmental actors seeking, through various ethical and legitimate and less than ethical and legitimate means, to fulfill their goals by exerting influence. Governmental authorities give the first priority in their activity to their own considerations. Should these actors have objectives to which they accord priority over other objectives, such as the uncovering of common denominators, such actors would employ their political means—namely, means with which they achieve influence—to realize their objectives, even if this led to the frustration of realizing that objective. The objective of discovering common denominators would be jeopardized if governmental authorities thought that the objective was incompatible with their priorities.

Because principles have their objective, subjective and normative aspects, they are subject to various interpretations. They have different concepts. All might agree on abstract principles, such as honor, dignity, contentment and progress, but people have different conceptions and interpretations of these principles. Because they are abstract, these principles may appear to be suitable as referential principles, but actually they may not be so, because of the differing interpretations, conceptions and "readings" of such principles. Should a point of reference be predicated on these principles only—without having the point of reference accommodating the difference of conception and interpretations of these principles—it becomes clear, when trying to apply them when conceived in a less abstract level in more specific and concrete social contexts, that that point of reference was not the final, clear-cut one.

Of the values for which we yearn and should yearn, as many other peoples do, are the values of freedom and democracy. Freedom and democracy have objective, subjective and normative aspects. These two values are colored with the social, economic and political circumstances which prevail in a society. By virtue of this, there should be various concepts of freedom and democracy. The differences in the concepts of freedom and democracy and of other values for which we yearn makes it necessary that our point of reference be one which does not restrict thought, or does so only to the necessary extent. According to this definition, a point of reference may be consent on the possibility of difference and disagreement and on the mutual conduct of human relations on the basis of this possibility; consent on eligibility to participate in dialogue not being dependent on lack of a difference. The more stable principles in the point of reference should be that others should not be boycotted or accused of disloyalty, on the grounds that they have a different opinion, and that a person should not arrogate to himself a greater right to express opinion than others. The basic premise of the point of reference is the possibility of the change of various points of departure and subjection of various concepts to various interpretations, except the above-mentioned basic principles.

What further mars intellectual communication is the effect of social and cultural conditioning on conceptual definition. This effect is manifested in the use of the same concepts that have different definitions and convey different meanings, and, conversely, the use of different expressions to convey almost identical meanings. For a man or a woman to be naked in public is a kind of exercise of the right to freedom in certain parts of the West. This behavior is regarded as a breach of public ethical order in Muslim countries. In such cases, intellectual communication could be improved by unifying the context of dialogue through the raising of the theoretical level of intellectual presentation.

Many of the social, cultural, economic and political institutions in the Arab world, as in the rest of the developing world, are in a state of change, by virtue of the social development through which the Arab people are passing. This process of change seems that it will take a relatively long time, because of our past and present political, economic and social experience, which has delayed our progress in these fields. This experience is characterized by strong contradictory cultural and political forces. Given this state of development, a point of reference should be formulated in such a way that it would not go ahead of the results of this development or interrupt or restrict it.

What contribute considerably to the multitude of interpretations and concepts of general principles are class affiliation, the cultural, educational and intellectual level, home upbringing, economic condition and the prevailing political environment. All these factors go a long way in determining understanding and interpretation of the general intellectual and value principles. Given the difference of these factors and of their strength, interpretations of these principles also differ, which shows that those principles are not suitable to be the final point of reference. To have a common point of reference, shared by all groups, would not necessarily mean agreement on the question under consideration or the lack of disagreement. Ideological difference or disagreement may exist, but this should not necessarily mean the lack of a point of reference, because a point of reference should encompass differences of ideology and thinking, and its intellectual scope should be wide enough to accommodate this difference. One of the functions of a point of reference is to achieve coexistence among the various groups in the shadow of difference and disagreement.

In societies there are groups with various intellectual and ideological interests and trends. These interests and trends have various requirements in the fields of public policy, life, economy and the general intellectual and value orientation of society. It is not allowed—from the perspective of the general interest of society—that any special point of reference of one of these groups be regarded as the general point of reference for society, because of the limited scope of these various points of reference of the groups.

These groups differ from each other in the extent of their influence on the life of society and state. It seems that of these groups, government is the most influential. Government, with its political authority, financial resources and military power, can exercise, and it does actually exercise, the largest influence on the life of society. In view of the fact that government is no more than one, though important, group in society and that it has ability to exert the largest influence on the life of society and state, and that the intellectual and value general point of reference for society should be wider than that of the government point of refer-ence, then caution should always be exercised against having the government point of reference dominate the general point of reference. Governmental excesses should always be curbed, and political, economic and legal strengthening of other groups in society should be undertaken so that the narrower governmen-tal point of reference is not imposed on those groups.

What would also increase the intensity of the crisis of a meaningful dialogue is for the government to organize the dialogue and to regulate it. That would be in stark contradiction with the concept of dialogue, being the free exchange of ideas, and with the existence of the notion of a point of reference which, by its defini-tion, does not allow for organization or regulation.

And even if all groups have agreed that a point of reference should be general principles, such an agreement would not mean that we, with such an agreement, have escaped the problematic aspect of the point of reference, and that is because general principles themselves are subject to various interpretations, because there are different concepts of one principle and because the intended significance of a principle changes with the change of time and place. In fact, the possibility of dif-ferent concepts and interpretations thereof requires conduct of dialogue in an attempt to reach results and conclusions of significance to various groups in soci-ety.

What facilitates arrival at a general point of reference is not to have a tradi-tional, but a liberated, thought; not to have a withdrawing or inverting thought but that which is characterized by what may be called centrifugal force. What is consistent with the method of thought which we are calling for is to tend to make assumptions in order to minimize for-granted axioms, not to understand what we are ignorant of as non-existent, not to be so zealous to ideas that no margin is left large enough to accommodate probability of error, to try to understand the opin-ions of others and not to believe that the correctness of the opinion of the other is the 'end of the world' for us.

In order to achieve a greater degree of dialogue and to facilitate reaching a point of reference, it is necessary that participants in the dialogue be at a higher level of education and knowledge, as both of these make a significant contribu-tion to providing ability to making dialogue revolve more around the thought emanating from one engaging in dialogue than around his personality. In other words, themes of discussion differ in the extent of one's subjectivity, beliefs and values. The higher the level of one's education and understanding, the abler is one to separate the theme from the self, and thus the role of thinking in dialogue increases. A higher level of education and knowledge possessed by those engaging in dialogue also make a significant contribute to providing ability to theorize, thus contributing to agreement on a point of reference. Theorization is general and explanatory intellectual articulation; through this articulation more subjective and less objective features of thought are avoided. These are the features which contribute to prevent reaching agreement on a general point of reference and for each of the parties to a dialogue to be entrenched behind its intellectual and ideological position.

What would further contribute to reaching a point of reference is democratization, which provides representation, freedom of expression of thought, and exercise of criticism and intellectual pluralism. Through democratization, the hands of the more influential and powerful groups, which seek to impose their own narrow and limited point of reference, would be restricted.

It is easier for people to agree on more abstract concepts; when a concept is used, the lower the level of abstraction the greater the likelihood of disagreement over its intended significance. And the contrary is true: namely, the higher is the level of abstraction the less likelihood is there of disagreement among people over its intended significance. This applies, of course, to the concept of point of reference, and concepts associated with it. Even if people agreed over an abstract concept of a point of reference, it would not be a full agreement when such in less abstract cases.

Related to the matter of conceptual abstraction is the difference in the extent conceptual abstraction and definiteness. People differ in the extent of abstraction or definiteness of their ideas. For intellectual communication to achieve maximum of effectiveness, ideas of parties attempting to engage in dialogue need to have reached the same, or almost the same, degree of abstraction and definiteness. Exchange of ideas between parties whose ideas have different levels of abstraction and definiteness contributes to the difficulty of engaging in effective dialogue and intellectual convergence.

One of the conditions needed to achieve dialogue is that of listening to what the other party has to say. The intellectual exchange involved in dialogue cannot be achieved without the parties transmitting at least some of their ideas to each other. In some cases one party, instead of listening, is busy, while the other party is speaking, with trying to rally his ideas and preparing to speak. This deprives him of the opportunity to understand what the other has to say. In this case, dialogue does not materialize, because of the lack of its constituents. Talk then becomes a mere expression of ideas. Such a situation does not lead to dialogue.

There are societies in which individuals regard dialogue as a sort of duel in which one is victorious and the other defeated—a sort of fight between two adversaries. In such societies, one attempting to engage in dialogue regards the proof of the fault of his ideas as a defeat that affects his status.

For further information, the following titles are provided: Rauf, Abdul, "Islam and the West—A Dialogue," Journal of Third World Studies, Spring 2001: State Power and Social Forces: Domination and Transformation in the Third World, ed. by Joel S. Migdal and others (Cambridge University Press, 1994); Third Intellectual Dialogue on Building Asia's Tomorrow, Bangkok, Thailand, June 2000 (Tokyo: Japan Center for International Exchange, 2000).

* The article was published in The Arab American Dialogue, Vol. 15, No. 3, Summer 2004.

Western Misconceptions of Third-World Cultural and Historical Context*

Third-World countries have suffered from a tendency in the West to depict them in abstractions. But no understanding of the policies and practices, be they social, economic or political, of Third-World peoples can be achieved without taking into account these peoples' own concrete experiences and cultural backgrounds. More abstract statements about peoples have been made at the expense of historical and cultural specificities, which are not properly spelled out.

The histories and cultures of peoples have been one of the most important factors in determining peoples' identities, values and aspirations. History and culture are now more relevant for a people's characterization of themselves in the Third World than in the West. Third-World peoples are now going through a stage in their existence where history and culture are more meaningful for their socio-economic development, for their nationhood, statehood and distinctness than history and culture are for Western countries. History and culture play a role in the conduct—official and unofficial—of Third-World countries bigger than that played by them in Western countries. Thus, history and culture deserve a bigger place in depicting, explaining and predicting conduct of Third-World countries than the place played by them in Western countries.

For a Western writer—whose knowledge of non-Western peoples and cultures may be questionable—to make a more abstract statement about a certain characteristic of Third-World peoples would be to run the risk of depriving himself or herself of the ability to understand, through proper analysis, the conduct of such peoples; with such abstraction, no sufficient account would be taken of the specific historical and cultural dimensions.

Analysts, mainly Western, have attempted to approach issues associated with development in Third-World countries using Western terms and concepts, such as Westernization, globalization and modernization. Many of these concepts, such as Westernization, are products of Western social, cultural, economic and historical background. As such, they are not universal; they are not universally relevant to the different background of Third-World countries. From such Western concepts, more specific historical and cultural dimensions of Third-World conduct are missing. Thus, such concepts are remarkable for their insensitivity to the culture and history of others.

It is not only that in the West there are many who show a tendency, for their own purposes, to make more abstract statements or generalizations. But, they also make such statements with much confidence and certainty, leaving no room for the possibility—indeed, the likelihood or even certainty—that they are misconceived.

In all countries, to varying degrees, it is the historical and, particularly, the cultural background which gives meaning to the way of life of a certain people. More abstract statements about a certain way of life or conduct ignore the historical and cultural connotations. Take, for example, the cultural, political, national and historical concept of 'honor,' which is a central element in Third-World political movements for liberation from foreign rule, dependency and want. To retain the true and intended meaning of this concept, it must stay within this Third-World political, national, cultural and historical context. One way to strip this concept of its nationally and politically important cultural and historical specificity would be to resort to a sort of abstraction by labeling acts of 'honor' as, say, 'practices.' This kind of abstraction is a useful tool for those in the West, who are not sympathetic, to say the least, to independence movements in the Third World. Such approach on the part of Westerners has created that cultural and political gap between the West and the Third World, as such an approach has made it more difficult for Westerners to understand political and cultural concepts drawn from Third-World backgrounds. By referring to acts of 'honor' as 'practices' one would be insensitive to particular cultural and historical backgrounds and values of other peoples.

By this approach, people in the West are kept in ignorance of Third-World affairs, and the thrust of the message contained in the context of 'honor' is lost. By this approach, history, politics, culture and behavior in the Third World cannot be understood. Unlike 'honor,' which is more concrete or less abstract culturally, politically, structurally and functionally, the expression of 'practice' is less concrete and more indefinite. Unlike the concept of 'honor,' it is not animated by the power of the cultural, historical and political reality. It is more colorless and neutral and less charged.

By subsuming acts of 'honor' under 'practices' one would make it more difficult to understand and explain Third-World reality by opening the door wide to a greater variety of interpretations than the more definite and concrete concept of 'honor.'

'Struggle' is another example. In the Third-World context, 'struggle' means a great deal historically, politically, nationally and culturally. For Third-World countries, struggle was one of the major instruments for such countries to achieve political independence, recover national honor and regain cultural identity. Struggle stands as a milestone in the recent history of Third-World peoples. 'Struggle' is a concept, a tool to explain and understand these peoples' recent history, life and affairs. To try to replace the term of 'struggle' with, say, term of 'violence' would be to substitute a more indefinite and abstract expression for the more definite and concrete one; the concreteness, definiteness and specificity of the concept of 'struggle' in the Third-World context would be lost. And to use the concept of 'violence' for 'struggle' would be to deprive seekers of knowledge of a grasp of Third World affairs and a means of understanding the nature of the national and political process in the Third World. Other examples would be to substitute 'extreme ideology' for 'nationalism,' and 'ramanticism' for 'attachment to a past glory.'

* The article was published in <u>The Arab American Dialogue</u>, Vol. 9, No. 4, April-May 1998.

Application of Technology as a Factor in Social Development*

Abstract

The article argues that application of technology would be instrumental in initiating or accelerating social development if those who apply the technology adopt attitudes and, hence, behavioral patterns characteristic of more developed societies, such as depersonalization, resulting from technology's positive response to the activator; conformity to synchronous timing, resulting from technology's non-compliance, while in activation, with any external factor; status differentiation, resulting from technology's relation to the individual occupying a certain status; and change in status hierarchy and non-conformism, resulting from technology's strengthening of professional functionalism.

Introduction

Technology is a tool, medium or instrument, in the sense that, through it, functions are performed. It performs functions in various social fields: political, economic, psychological, military, administrative and others.

Focusing on the developing countries, the paper at hand sets as its objective to show that application of technology would be instrumental in initiating or accelerating social development by making people applying it adopt attitudes and, hence, behavior, characteristic of more developed countries, such as depersonalization, conformity to synchronous timing, status differentiation and alteration of status hierarchy, and non-conformism. An attitude is defined here as an interpretation of experience, or definition of a situation. (1)

Depersonalization

Technology is an impersonal instrument, in the sense that, by its nature, it listens and obeys to the operator, and it is activated or deactivated, regardless of the one that activates or deactivates it, be he a man, woman, child, or monkey or cat. It is blind to values external to it. It performs uniformly with no particular attention, reference or consideration to human values as such. Because its activity is impersonal, technology responds positively to any activator.

This attribute of technology would make the applicant more conscious or less unconscious of the existence of personal relations between human beings and things. Such a change would have an attitudinal and, hence, behavioral, influence on its applicant.

Conformity to Synchronous Timing

The concept of time is an inherent value or attribute in technological application. Technology, in particular its modern variety, is activated by certain speeds. Once turned on at a certain speed, no personal, interfering or intrusive factor can change it. Technology, in its given speed, while in activation, does not 'comply' with, or 'listen' to, any personal, intrusive or external factor. With the activation of technology, an activator from any country comes to realize or to better appreciate the concept of time. An activator, knowing that after a certain hour an industrial facility would explode if a certain switch is not turned on or off, and that he would be liable to lose his job should this happen, would make a more conscious effort to get to the premises on time.

Status Differentiation

With the application of technology, people get a better idea about status differentiation. The most basic unit of human structure is status. Social structure refers to the recurring patterns of behavior that create relationships among individuals and groups within a society. (2) There are various definitions of the term 'status.' Status as is used in this paper refers to a person's membership in a social category. (3) A medical doctor, a patient, the chief of a tribe, a story-teller, a pilot and an engineer are examples of status.

A role is a set of norms attached to a status. (4) Persons who fit a certain status ir belong to a category generally behave in predictable ways partly due to the fact that there are social norms that define appropriate behavior for people in that category. (5) There is, however, a 'role distance,' namely, that the behavior of the person is not always in accordance with the role attached to him. (6)

There are less clearly defined boundaries for a given status occupied by an individual in less-developed countries. One act by an individual in these countries may originate from his occupying more than one status. An order by a chief of a village, for instance, may be obeyed because the chief also occupied other statuses, such as head of a family, a landowner, and an opinion leader. This phenomenon of multi-status action does most certainly exist in all societies, but it is more pronounced and prevalent in the less-developed ones.

The application of technology involves a functional relationship between the given technology and the human being. In performing its function vis-à-vis the human being, the technology relates to him as occupying a differentiated status, a status differentiated from other statuses. It relates to him as an individual occupying a certain status, and excludes other statuses he may occupy. An airplane, for example, would be performing its function as a vehicle of flight only when an individual occupies the status of a pilot, even though he may also be a tribal chief, a poet or a traditional story-teller. For the airplane to carry out the function of flying, all of the other statuses are irrelevant. Through this status differentiation in the relationship between technology and the human being, the latter comes to realize or to better realize the existence of the concept of status differentiation. This better realization would have an altering influence on attitude which, consequently, would affect the individual's behavior in society. By making an individual internally more functionally differentiated, application of technology would make him more developed.

With status differentiation, an individual should develop greater freedom in assuming attitudes, namely, interpretation and definition of situations, and in interpreting and defining human values.

There is also a relationship between values becoming more abstract and behavioral change. With the passage of time, values become more abstract. With that greater freedom and with values becoming more abstract, an individual possessing a certain status should become more amenable to individual variation and the willingness to more or change.

Change in Status Hierarchy

It is not only that, as above mentioned, every individual occupies at the same time a number of statuses, but also a hierarchy of statuses does exist in every individual. In setting the order of statuses in such hierarchy, non-professional values will have a varying impact. This impact has a strong say in making the order of such statuses hierarchical or vertical. The less such an impact is, the less hierarchical that order it. Just as the application of technology improves professional functionalism, such application increases the impact of the professional impact. Such a change should lead to a less hierarchical order of statuses, hence a more general and egalitarian attitude.

Non-Conformism

Conformism may be defined as behavior according to a set of social rules universally accepted by a given social group. These rules, being a product of various social, cultural and historical factors, may be 'good' or 'bad.' Usually, members of such groups conform to the groups' norms.

In the human application of technology, or in the relationship between the individual and technology in activation, there is very little, if any, relevance for social conformism. Because of the non-social and impersonal nature of technological activation, there is no consideration for social conformism. One, in applying technology, is concerned less with social conformism than with the requirements emanating from the non-socially-conditioned activation of the machine. Such an applicant would be bound to develop a mental differentiation between social conformism and technological conformism. This differentiation would initiate an attitudinal alteration, would initiate an alteration of attitude toward social conformism and technological conformism. A mental differentiation between both types of conformism and an alteration of attitude towards them, as a result of such differentiation, would well lead to a behavioral change on the part of the applicant of technology, from social conformism to broader ideas, allowing for a behavior not derived solely from such conformism but also from the requirements of technological application.

The behavior of an individual in a social category or status generally represents conformity to the expectations of others with respect to how an individual in that category should behave. It needs to be mentioned that the expectations of other people differ. 'Role conflict' is a situation where a person is torn between inconsistent expectations. For an individual to occupy statuses, with conflicting norms governing the various statuses, involve role conflict. Role conflict may arise as a result of a status change or the acquisition of a new status. Roles governing the former and new statuses might well be in conflict. In situations of role conflict, an individual occupying one or more statuses would be bound to decide which role to give preference. In such a decision, functional and professional status differentiation, achieved by the application of technology, would have a considerable effect on the occupant when he comes to decide on the preferences he would give to the conflicting roles, thus possibly weakening the statuses which are not functional and professional.

Individuals conform to norms attached to their statuses for various reasons, one more important of which is that individuals become identified with their statuses. As the application of technology makes status more functionally and professionally bound and accentuates functional and professional relevance, then such application weakens one's identification with some of his ascriptively-achieved statuses. This change strengthens one's identification with some of his earned statuses, thus leading to decreased conformity to norms governing ascribed statyses and, consequently, to change in his behavior.

Endnotes

1. See W.I. Thomas and Dorothy S. Thomas, <u>The Child in America</u> (New York: Knopf, 1928).

2. See William Kornblum, <u>Sociology in a Changing World</u> (New York: Holt, Rinehart and Winston, 1988), p. 59.

3. Jerry D. Rose, <u>Introduction to Sociology</u>, 2nd ed. (Chicago: Rand McNally, 1974), p. 93.

4. <u>Ibid</u>., p. 64.

5. <u>Ibid</u>.

6. See, for example, Erving Goffman, <u>Encounters: Two Studies in the Sociology of Interaction</u> (Indianapolis: Bobbs-Merrill, 1961).

* The paper was presented at the 20th Annual Third World Conference, April 6-9, 1994, Congress Hotel, Chicago, IL.

Factors for the Strength and Weakness of States in the Developing World, with a Particular Reference to South-West Asia

An Abstract

Statehood was attained between the 1940s and the 1960s for most of the developing countries. Before attaining that status, most of these countries were ruled by Great Britain, France, Spain and other European states.

A number of factors, such as tribalism, feudalism, a strong sense of family and ethnic affiliation, globalization, religion, sectarianism, have weakened the legitimacy of state authority, whereas other factors, such as national movements and a more effective communications system have strengthened the legitimacy of such authority. Often, some of these contradictory factors were at play at the same time. The extent and direction of their influence depended on their dynamic interrelationships and on their interrelationships with the cultural, economic and political setting.

The objective of this paper is to study the roles played by those factors that have the effect of weakening or strengthening the legitimacy of state authority.

The method used in this study is textual and historical. The dynamic relations between tribalism, feudalism, ethnic, religious, sectarian and family affiliation, and ideology mainly during the twentieth century are studied, using national and international sources dealing with political, religious, cultural and economic matters.

The conclusion of this paper is that, in spite of the strengthened status of the state as an institution, it still lacks that self-confidence discernible in political entities in Europe that have a longer tradition of statehood.

Factors That Weaken the Legitimacy
of State Authority

The question of the state in the developing countries, its concept, authority, legitimacy and history has received significant attention in socio-political, cultural and historical studies in the West as well as the Third World. More studies need to be made in order to further elucidate some aspects of this question, in particular the fear expressed by Third World students of politics and sociology concerning factors that are likely to lead to further splitting of a number of Third World states. These factors include, but are not limited to, foreign intervention, linguistic, religious or sectarian divisions. Various precedents of state fragmentation and secession strengthen this fear.

There were large and centralized states in ancient and medieval times, such as ancient Egypt, the Fatimid state with Cairo as its capital, the Umayyad state with Damascus as its capital, and the Abbasid state with Baghdad as its capital.

In the developing countries state authority is both strong and weak. There are two kinds of trends that have contradictory effects: one is centrifugal; it weakens state legitimacy. The other one is centripetal and unifying; it strengthens state legitimacy. Before going further, definitions of a number of concepts are needed. The author of this paper has adopted these definitions. In 1918, Max Weber defined state as "a human community that (successfully) claims *the monopoly of the legitimate use of physical force* within a given territory…. The right to use physical force is ascribed to other institutions or to individuals only to the extent to which the state permits it. The state is considered the sole source of the 'right' to use violence."(1) Weber continued to say, "Hence, 'politics' for us means striving to share power or striving to influence the distribution of power, either among states or among groups within a state."(2) 'State' thus may be defined as a set of political institutions in a society, that is, the institutions that deal, in Lasswell's phrase, with questions of "who gets what, when and how."(3) In any society, politics determines, in Lasswell's words, "who gets what, when, and how." Everywhere the basis of politics is competition for power. Power is the ability to control others' behavior out of their volition or in spite of them. To be powerful is to have the ability to have your way even if others oppose it.(4) Authority is defined as institutionalized power, that is to say, power whose exercise is governed by the norms and status of organizations.(5)

The state in the traditional sense or before globalization is the largest territory within which political institutions can operate without having its right to govern, that is, sovereignty, being challenged. Under certain circumstances the state dele-

gates to other institutions, for instance, municipal, county and provincial authorities, monopoly over the use of force. The state gains this monopoly, the ultimate
source of its power to influence the behavior of the populace, from their belief in
the legitimacy of the state's possession of such power.

The various factors that either weaken or strengthen the state's legitimacy are
religion, sectarianism, communications, tribalism, ethnicity and others. The
influence of these factors, which date back many centuries, depends also on the
dynamic relationships among these institutions themselves and between them
and the state authority.

The factors that weaken the legitimacy of state authority include excessive
individualism (among some populations, such as sections of the Arab population), a strong sense of family affiliation (in Arab and non-Arab countries), religion (in this case, it weakens the legitimacy of the authority of the national or
secular state), feudalism (in some countries), tribalism, ethnicity, partisanship
and ideology (such as communism), patriarchy, excesses of practices by state
authorities (these excesses include dictatorship, oppression, totalitarianism,
authoritarianism) and the newness of many states.

Patriarchy, tribalism, a strong sense of family affiliation, feudalism, partisanship and religion compete with the state authority over people's allegiance. A person's allegiance is given not to the state, but to these factors. An indication of the
fact that allegiance is the focus of competing value systems and that religious affiliation has a say in where allegiance lies is that in a number of states, such as
Morocco, Egypt and Ethiopia, religion was the driving factor for Jews who immi-
grated to Israel. Islamic affiliation weakens allegiance to the authority of the
national or secular state. But, should the state be Islamic, then religious affiliation
would strengthen the state authority. The matter of allegiance has come into
sharper focus with the growth of Islamic movements since the 1950s. With this
growth, the religious or sectarian dimension coincided with internal cohesion or
lack of it in a number of states as well as with inter-state relations.

Ethnicity and religious and sectarian affiliation have been an important factor
in arousing fear of state splintering, and, sometimes, in competing with the state
for people's allegiance. In many developing states, there is in each state more than
one ethnic group and an affiliation with more than one religion and sect. In
many of these states, there is no identity between the nation-state and the ethnic
composition of the population. For instance, there are Kurdish political movements that strive to establish an independent state of Kurdistan comprising
Kurds living in parts of Iraq, Turkey, Iran and Syria. Berbers in Algeria and
Morocco have a strong ethnic identity. Maronites of Lebanon have a strong sec-

tarian-ethnic consciousness. Because of the relative weakness of the state, the cementing or splintering effect of ethnic identity and of religious and sectarian affiliation on the state is stronger. Various internal and external, regional and international, ideological-cultural and political factors have determined whether such an identity and affiliation had a splintering or cementing effect on the state.

A consensus between state authority and the people on quite a few issues in many fields is lacking. Under the rubric of ideology might fall the often wide gap that exists between the position taken by the state authority and peoples' positions towards such issues as relations with Israel (in the case of the Arab states, in particular), policies pursued by certain Western states on the international scene, globalization, modernity on the Western model, secularization and internal socio-economic policies. In many of these states there is a wide gap between the state authority and a combination of these and other issues. This lack of consensus has weakened and is still weakening the legitimacy of state authority.

Related to the lack of consensus is the lack of openness on the part of the state authority to various intellectual currents, in particular those that deal with matters of the economy, belief and freedom of expression. Lack of democracy, in particular political democracy, to which the issue of lack of freedom of expression is intrinsically related, has been and still is a major factor of disagreement between the state authority and the people. Lack of democracy has been and still is a very significant factor in lessening the legitimacy of state authority in the eyes of the people, particularly the intellectuals.

In a number of Muslim communities, state authority was opposed or rejected by Islamists because of the Western ideological baggage carried along with some features of modernization on the Western model. Secularization, materialism, excessive consumerism, usury, sexual permissiveness and other ideological features that came with the Western model of modernity were rejected by the Islamists and not only by them. They opposed a state model that was associated with such features.

Lack of democracy makes it easier for state authority to conduct its affairs in a way lacking in transparency. This has made it easier for corruption to spread in the political, financial, mercantile and administrative fields in certain states and/ or certain cases.

In such cases, there is no adequate communication between state authority and the populace. This is related to such factors as the one mentioned earlier, namely, lack of openness on the part of the authority to prevailing intellectual currents. This state of affairs has contributed to the authority's belief, of which more educated people are aware, that it is above criticism and beyond accountability, and that it, namely the authority, has a right to censor people's writings and readings. All of these factors have contributed to weakening the legitimacy of the authority.

Legitimacy of the state authority has been adversely affected by the adoption by state authorities of a policy favoring certain developments and phenomena, such as globalization, entering into alliance, secularization, social and economic structural adjustment, without being sufficiently sensitive to the needs, wishes and attitudes of the people.

Authoritarian, oppressive, suppressive, dictatorial and intrusive practices by state authority have had an adverse effect on state legitimacy. There is governmental corruption. There is a considerable degree of social and cultural oppression sponsored by the state. The state is not performing the bigger, more generalized role that it can, or is expected, to perform. The state is not the state for all of its citizens. People are not treated as citizens but as subjects. Benefits from the state are confined to certain groups. Some of the services and benefits that residents usually obtain in the West from their states often are obtained by inhabitants in developing countries from institutions other than the state and, consequently, their allegiance is given more to those institutions than to the state. This socio-political culture has been a major reason for the lack of a genuine political participation by the people. Even though there may be parliaments, parties and elections, no real democracy was practiced. Such institutions were facades of democracy. Decisions that have bearing on the fate of the state and the people were not a result of a democratic process, but were taken by the few who rule. In a number of cases, spontaneity has been a major feature of decision-making and action. Such phenomena and practices have caused shrinkage and eventual disappearance of many people's acceptance of state authority. They have diminished many people's compliance with the state's regulations and have alienated such people.

The effect of such practices on the legitimacy of the state authority has been stronger when directed against certain institutions in some countries, such as affiliations to certain religious, ethnic or language groups. Because of the belief and ideological contents of such institutions, groups belonging to such institutions have shown a very strong sensitivity to such practices. The actual embodiment of such sensitivity took the form of protest against state authority and disrespect of its legitimacy.

Tribalism, feudalism, a strong sense of family affiliation and others that compete with the state over allegiance of the populace are evident in various parts of the developing countries. Modernizing influences in the socio-political and economic fields initially and for some time did contribute to some people's adopting a more favorable attitude to the idea of the state as the focus of allegiance and to initial weakening of allegiance to these institutions. However, seeing the wide gap in position between state authority and the populace, witnessing the insensitivity on the part of that authority to the people's needs, witnessing the oppression, authoritarianism and corruption and witnessing the lack of freedom, these segments of the populace were inhibited from further development of their belief in the state's right to use force, their willingness to accept that right and their allegiance to it, and were prompted to assert their already existing allegiances to the tribe, family, religion and the local community.

Miserable social conditions prevailing in the overwhelming majority of the developing countries have the effect of weakening the state and legitimacy of its authority. There is abject poverty among a very high percentage of the peoples. Illiteracy is rampant. Chronic and fatal diseases are widespread. There is a very high percentage of unemployment. Income is very limited. Some essential products are very expensive. In many countries, social security and unemployment benefits are lacking. In many places medical services do not exist. People generally need welfare, or an assisting, state in case of need. When a person, especially if old or handicapped, faces a hardship, he/she experiences a real dilemma, as often there is no state social institution to take good care of him/her. This did not help state authority to solidify its legitimacy. It militated against whatever measures of legitimacy were in existence. These conditions have the effect of leading many people to direct or re-direct their allegiance to closer and smaller groups as a source of assurance and help, such as the tribe, family, local community and religion, which are willing to provide him with whatever support they might have. This, in turn, has strengthened the standing of these smaller groups. His belief, whether on concrete or imagined grounds, of these groups' ability to meet his needs has made him feel more distant from the state and more attached to his respective group or groups.

The position taken by the government towards foreign intervention has also been a factor that weakened the legitimacy of the government authority. One of the main characteristics of the prevailing world financial and economic system is that within its framework there are actors, including foreign states, corporations, whether domestic or transnational, that exercise, directly or indirectly, control—be it financial, military or political—over other countries, mainly the developing countries. Pretexts of protection of human rights and of certain minorities have traditionally been used by certain actors to justify their intervention in the internal affairs of developing countries. Through their hold over the mechanisms of control, these actors, that sought and still seek to promote their financial, political and strategic interests, achieved a great success in realizing these interests. Globalization is one of the mechanisms of control. One of the main features of globalization is that the market is almost the only regulator of relations between political, financial and economic institutions, and that the influence of such a market is extended globally. Globalization is also characterized by the quickness of overt or covert transfer and use of money with no respect for sovereign privileges of states, including their territorial boundaries, thus depriving them of the ability to fully prevent such transfers and use.

Through the use of such mechanisms, these actors have been a major factor in making the economies of such countries dependent on foreign economies. In the free financial market, peoples of these countries have experienced tough times in competing with foreign actors. Through the use of the mechanisms of control, foreign actors have contributed significantly to the reduction of the amount of exported products from these countries and to the considerable lowering of the prices of such products and, at the same time, these actors have increased the volume and prices of exported products to these countries, thus causing very negative effects on the weakened economies of the latter countries; the value of their currencies has been lowered; transfer of advanced technology needed for economic and social development has been restricted. These factors have contributed to heightening inflation, adding to make their budget deficit, increasing their indebtedness, thus making it more difficult for them to purchase foreign products needed for economic and social growth.

All of these developments have increased the peoples' resentment towards, and dissatisfaction with, the governments, leading to weaken the legitimacy of their authority.

This globalized world system has been largely responsible for the developing countries' need for loans, some of which they secured from international lending institutions. Being a part of this system, these institutions have the practice of making grant of loans conditional on these countries' taking certain domestic economic, financial and social measures, including primarily restructuring and adjustment. These measures included privatization of ownership of institutions, limiting of expenditure on social projects and cancellation of government financial subsidies with respect to some vital commodities such as bread, raising of taxes, encouragement of the adoption of concepts as work efficiency and rationalization of employment policies.

The results of such measures were mixed. Here, I am focusing my attention on those results that have exacerbated the peoples' resentment. With costly loan servicing, these loans further weakened the economies of these countries. They have consumed the lion share of their meager earnings. Restructuring measures have aggravated the already miserable living conditions of many segments of the population. Through the terms of these loans, which also included social and economic restructuring, foreign actors have considerably affected the economic structure inside the recipient countries.

These overall developments have contributed significantly to the economic, cultural and political weakening of the developing countries. This has slowed down or held back their economic, cultural, social and democratic development, leading to further aggravation of the peoples' economic hardships, a lowering of their already low standard of living, making them more dispossessed and miserable and the spread of poverty and malnutrition. This worsening condition of marginalization and poverty has and is causing disappointment, resentment, anger, and protest on the part of the affected peoples, leading to the corrosion of the legitimacy of the state authority.

What made the developing countries' resentment more acute is the attempt made by certain Western parties to impose on them the West's model of development. "Developing countries" in the economic and cultural fields does not mean backward countries in the historical perspective. These countries had in the past grown and developed in the fields of social and natural sciences, philosophy and establishment of administrative, state and empire structures. They have created beautiful and humanistic cultures and great civilizations.

In each state, besides the governments there are very influential groups with strong financial interests. There is a strong alliance between government organs and such groups. Both these organs and groups seek to make big and fast profits. Of the activities carried out by such organs and groups to accumulate wealth are monopoly over vital economic sectors, such as export, import, distribution and marketing of commodities, and implementation of governmental and public projects; they play the role of middleman in the sale or purchase of such products as weapons in return for a large commission. Through arrangements between such organs and groups they reap great profits, with out paying adequate attention to the interests of the suffering masses. In such activities, government organs and their allied groups have received and continue to receive the backing of foreign actors who have an economic interest in making big profits from financial and economic arrangements with internal governmental organs and interest groups.

Such arrangements have aggravated the poverty and suffering of the population. Inflation became more acute. Unemployment and high prices of essential commodities became more widespread. As a result, the budgetary deficit grew sharper. All these developments have weighed on the people, especially children, the elderly, women, the handicapped and unskilled laborers.

In this overall situation foreign actors do influence the internal policy of the developing countries. Foreign actors have a major influence on the composition of government cabinets and on appointments for senior positions in the economy, the banking system and the mass media. Such influence has been of such a far-reaching extent that it may be described as an intervention in the formulation or direction of that policy. This way, legitimacy of state authority is challenged and weakened in the eyes of the population.

As we have stated earlier, those who hold the reigns of power in the developing countries have interests in continued retention of power and in promoting their economic interests. Because of the foreign actors' being an important source of support for those who wield such power, the latter have been more willing to make their policy obedient, or less opposed, to the directions of the foreign actors in some basic aspects of their internal and external policies, or soften and attenuate them, so that such policies would be more accommodating to the objectives of those actors. What made this obedience more forthcoming is the mounting foreign debt of these countries and their increasing economic dependence on such actors. In view of the need of those actors for backing from those holding the reigns of power in order to achieve the formers' financial and strategic objectives, there has emerged between the two parties closeness, understanding, mutual backing, coordination or alliance. This has further weakened the legitimacy of state authority.

The inability of the developing countries to repay their foreign debts with their exorbitant costs has increased the effectiveness of the foreign actors' influence on the governments of those countries, thus contributing greatly to the further harnessing and subjection of those governments to foreign policies. This increased subjection is translated into the governments' formulation of internal and external policies and taking of measures intended to accommodate and meet the policies and priorities of the foreign actors. This has meant that the governments become—out of their desire or in spite of them—internal intermediaries or agents for foreign actors.

The original intention of the state authority was that it should be the authority of the state in which it is practiced. Even though state authority is certainly and naturally—because of its being a part of regional and international environments—exposed to various foreign or internal influences, it is incompatible with the general and usual concept of state authority to have it inordinately directed by foreign influences or to be directed by foreign forces more than by internal forces.

With this foreign exposure and subjection the structure of the state changes. In this case, state authority virtually ceases to freely practice its primary function, namely, to preserve and protect the state's existence, territory and people.

Factors That Strengthen the Legitimacy of State Authority

In this section, factors that have the effect of strengthening states will be dealt with briefly. One of these factors has to do with Muslim-Arab states. In these states, Islam has performed the important function of expressing a form of ethnic and national self-awareness. Before the advent of Islam, Arab states existed in this peninsula and in the northern and north-western areas bordering it. Besides the spiritual, ethical and social functions, Islam unified the Arab tribes in the Arabian peninsula into one Arab-Islamic state.

Furthermore, there are two kinds of factors responsible for the emergence of states with a centralized authority: One group is that of mercantile civilizations, where certain cities play the role of channels that preserve information and material exchange that is needed for sustainable life. Trade expansion and the need for preservation of its vital routes require, at a certain stage, going beyond the confines of tribal, ethnic or religious division, and beyond the close-in, isolated cities.

In fact, the great volume of trade exchange over great distances create, with repetition and with needs generated by such repetition, increasingly strong links that establish the basis for the spread of trans-tribal, trans-ethnic and trans-religious authority, which constitutes a source of general interest for all sections of society.

The second kind of factors relates to the riverine civilizations. Because of life's dependence on rivers, such as the Euphrates, Tigris and the Nile, the state had imposed a strict centralized system of irrigation. This, in turn, makes necessary the existence of a strong political entity. The emergence of such a centralized state pre-supposed development of agriculture, methods of construction, mathematics and understanding of irrigation geography. In other words, it pre-supposed a civilizational advance that constituted a basis for the development of a centralized state in riverine civilizations. The riverine factor still has an effect in the maintenance of a centralized state authority in a number of states, such as Egypt.

Historically, a number of centralized states expanded into a far-flung empire. This was a source of internal and external weakness: another state, in competition with that empire and feeling threatened by it, might unleash a war against it. This was bound to result in weakening the empire economically and militarily, and in the ceding of some territory or putting an end to its existence.

In such an empire, the capital city was far away from outlaying areas, thus making the central authority less effective in administering and organizing state affairs and in ruling peoples living on the fringes of the empire. As a result, revolts against the central authority broke out. Constant efforts by the central authority to quell rebellions weakened the state authority, and the state itself, militarily and economically, and tempted strong neighboring states to attack that empire, in particular in case the rebellious groups sought assistance from the neighboring states. For example, the Muslim army, under the command of 'Amr Ibn Al-'As, who was directed by the Caliph in Medina to conquer Egypt, was assisted by the Egyptian Christian Copts who suffered maltreatment under the authority of the vast Byzantine Empire. Other examples are provided by the history of the Umayyad, Abbasid and Ottoman states.

In many instances, empires, centralized or otherwise, were states with dependent territories. The organic relations that we discern in a riverine state, that pull parts of the state together, are lacking in relations between an empire and its dependent territories. Instead of such relations, in the case of empires, relations between an empire and its dependencies are often dependent on military coercion. Separation or removal of parts of the empire and independence of their governors from the center were relatively easy.

The centralized states in the 19th and 20th centuries, such as the Wahhabi state in the Arabian peninsula, the Safavid state in Iran and the state of Egypt under the rule of Muhammad 'Ali drew partly on the strength of the traditional centralized state which had its roots in ancient or medieval times.

What have contributed to some degree of cohesion of the state are cultural factors, such as a common language, history, customs and traditions, and civilizational affiliation. These factors had their impact in the past and still retain their strength. External forces that accompany foreign intervention, cultural invasion and globalization have weakened these factors. Under constant pressure from these forces it would be difficult for such continuity to survive.

Economic links between the Arab states and the world market are getting stronger. The volume of trade exchange between them and foreign, mainly Western, countries is considerable and increasing. These links have made it more difficult to realize the pan-Arab state. This difficulty was bound to have the effect of the strengthening of the non-pan-Arab state. The dependent capitalist development of this state has been a major factor in such states' economies being structurally integrated with the globalized world market. This integration generates forces that are opposed to the formation of the Arab state at the broad Arab level. Besides long traditions and history, the non-pan-Arab state is founded on an agricultural base and foreign market relations. These smaller Arab states would likely have perished had it not been for the existence of relatively strong Arab states on the regional level, and for the existence of the system of international relations which, because of its interests, constitutes a factor for protection. The lack of a unified all-Arab market is a factor in preventing establishment of a pan-Arab state. A component of this system is globalization promoted by Western states. The emergence of a pan-Arab state would have been made easier with the creation of a unified all-Arab market. Because of internal, regional and international political, strategic and economic factors, however, this market is lacking.

There have been circumstances that further strengthened state authority vis-à-vis society and contributed significantly to the control of society. They included the priority and support given by national movements for the idea of statehood in their struggle against foreign rule and for political independence. For instance, the Arab national movement in the Fertile Crescent, in the late 19th century and during the first half of the 20th century, called for political independence of the Arab lands. This priority and support came at the expense of internal non-state organizations and institutions. From the 1940s, and in some cases from the turn of the century, those movements were seeking to end foreign rule and to gain political independence for their lands. This control has been a major factor in eliminating and preventing the growth of certain non-state organizations or institutions. These movements viewed some organizations as an obstruction to the achievement of their objective. For example, some movements fought the *zawaya*, namely, religious orders in North Africa. Had such organizations and institutions continued to exist, they would have had some influence in curbing the excesses of state organs.

Excesses of state organs could be curtailed by the emergence of the middle class, usually comprising such professionals as engineers, physicians, accountants, lawyers, journalists, professors and businessmen, who can form professional associations. The emergence of the middle class and such associations could be encouraged by combating poverty, disease and illiteracy and by dissemination of education, access to information sources and raising of consciousness. There would be a higher likelihood that members of the middle class and of these associations could do their jobs independent of the state organs and would not rely for their livelihood on the state organs, thus being more able to protect their rights and to voice their ideas with more confidence and freedom. So far, the middle class and civil professional associations have not emerged in many developing countries, and where they emerged, they are still not strong enough to influence state actions and policies.

Had the state in the developing world not weakened these associations, they might well have taken a stronger position against foreign actors and to have lent their political, financial and moral support to the state vis-à-vis these actors. State organs would have been able to use such associations in confronting some foreign pressures.

Foreign actors, being opposed to the emergence of strong states, acted to prevent the emergence of such associations or to weaken them. Hence, the convergence of interests between state organs and foreign actors often emerged to act against such associations.

Endnotes

1. H. Gerth and C. W. Mills, <u>From Max Weber: Essays in Sociology</u> (New York: Oxford University Press, 1958), p. 78; emphasis in original.

2. <u>Ibid</u>.

3. Harold D. Lasswell, <u>Politics: Who Gets What, When and How</u> (New York: McGraw-Hill, 1936).

4. C. W. Mills, <u>The Sociological Imagination</u> (New York: Oxford University Press, 1959).

5. William Kornblum, <u>Sociology in a Changing World</u> (New York: Holt, Rinehart and Winston, 1988), p. 439.

Socio-Political Oppression and Physical and Intellectual Exile, With a Particular Reference to the Developing Countries*

A state of exile and a state of at-homeness or belonging, which not infrequently are a result or a by-product of a socializational, cultural and mental process, can be physical-geographical, mental or both. Being in a state of exile may be voluntary or involuntary, volitional or forced. Emigration, immigration, imprisonment, displacement, homelessness, estrangement, alienation, disconnectedness, separation and isolation are sorts of either physical or metaphorical exile or both real and metaphorical exile at the same time. (1) States of exile and of at-homeness can exist with respect to the family, community, people, country or continent and also with respect to the self.

Interaction of Factors of Exile

Mental and physical states of exile and of at-homeness are a result of one or more of the following varied circumstances and conditions: a psychological state or mood, one's life experiences, financial and economic situation, socio-cultural, including political, circumstances, intellectual and emotional leanings, one's romantic or realistic view of the world and others. (2)

These different factors or sources are in constant interaction. They are also constantly interacting with the person concerned. As these factors are in constant interaction, they reinforce or weaken each other and vary in their intensity or presence. Because of the complex nature of the interrelationships of these factors and between them and the person concerned, the process might not consummate itself, and it may be lengthy or enduring.

A state of exile consists of centrifugal, centripetal or neutral forces. People with different ages, genders, personalities, life experiences and awareness differ one from the other in the weight of these forces in their attitudes. People's attitudes are, in a sense, a result of a blend of real and imagined perception, which determine the strength of the presence of the centripetal, centrifugal and neutral forces in a person's attitude. As life experiences change with a maturing age, the strength of the presence of these forces changes, with a more real and realistic perception probably acquiring a stronger presence in this structure. If this happens, factors that lead to a state of exile would change, thus bringing a change in the states of exile. Hence, this change in the strength of the presence of the three forces, following a change in the blend of imagined and real perceptions, provides a room for a shift from the range of a state of belonging to the range of a state of exile and vice versa.

Factors of exile and at-homeness might move in contrasting directions. Consequently, these states of exile and of at-homeness undergo constant changes with varying intensity and speed. This means that these states are not absolute, but relative. Thus, in one individual there can be one or more than one source of exile or disconnectness in co-existence with one or more than once source of at-homeness or connectedness. In this case, both kinds of sources would highly likely to clash leading to one of the two groups of sources to have the upper hand. Also, one might be in a state of intellectual and emotional exile from a certain place and, in the passage of time, with changing psychological and mental conditions and changing cultural and political circumstances, that state of emotional exile would be pulling to return, physically or metaphorically, to the "home" or the "homeland," whereas being still there, the state of intellectual exile will continue with its pressing in the direction away from the abandoned, previous "home."

Politics Involves Exertion of Influence

Politics has to do with influence. In any political context there is an influencer and an influencee, be they an individual, a family, a group, a tribe, a people or an empire. This influence pervades, though with varying degrees of intensity, all fields of life. There are various sources of influence. Of these sources, governmental influence probably is the strongest. If not the strongest, it is one of the strongest factors that creates for the individual a state of exile. (3)

Exile Indicates a Need for Change

To be in a state of exile suggests that a need or a desire is sensed to change, innovate and create. Manifestations of states of exile are the sense of the need and of the desire to change, innovate and create. A writer's sense of the need to express his/her criticism, disapproval and condemnation of prevailing conditions in whatever domain is a sort of estrangement or exile. A tendency to revolt or the sense of the need to revolt is another manifestation of the state of exile from a certain condition or a setting. By resorting to revolt one's self is positioned in a state of exile from whatever is revolted against. Displacement, dispossession, transfer of native peoples are phenomena that African and Palestinian poets, such as Mahmood Darwish, Samih al-Qasim and Jamal Qa'war, have revolted against. (4) These phenomena are the domains from which writers and poets have placed themselves in a state of exile.

Exile and Writing

As exile and other related conditions are a result of the lack of individual control over policy formulation, government practices and socio-economic developments, then writing, especially writing to the self, a monologue or a memoir, where a considerable degree of control by the writer is exercised, is a way to have a "homeland" or to stay "at home." (5) Because the worlds, spaces, imagery and freedom which belles-lettres, especially poetry, provide, literary figures have a strong sense of belonging to his/her home, namely, belles-lettres.

Governmental Policies and Exile

One can be in a condition of exile even where he/she is still physically living in the birthplace, whether in the family, tribe, quarter, village, town, country or region. In many countries, identity is shaped and recognized not by universal criteria, such as equal citizenship, equality before law, state for all of its citizens, political participation, but by restrictive particularistic criteria, such as class, religious, sectarian, ethnic, race, gender and linguistic affiliations. These affiliations make a difference in terms of the treatment by governmental organs of these groups. This particularistic attitude on the part of government has created a condition of alienation and exile for the followers of these groups within the country of birth. (6) An example of internalized exile is the sense of estrangement and disconnectedness many intellectuals in the Arab world (7) as well as the rest of the developing world have because of the deteriorating political, economic and social conditions internally and in the international arena.

Availability of Places of Exile is a Source of Contentment

The availability of places of exile, geographical or metaphorical, is a source of contentment on the part of those who, for some reason or the other, although are undergoing certain feelings of lack of satisfaction, have not entered a state of exile. The availability of places of exile can reassure such people that in case their psychological and cultural absorptive capacity cannot accommodate the current initial lack of satisfaction, they can move to the state of exile. (8)

The availability of places of exile can provide the "candidates" to enter a state of exile with some additional resources to try to cope or interact with the nascent or emerging dissatisfaction. This interaction might end with this person's ability to overcome the factors that would lead to the state of exile.

State of Exile and Gender

Men are physically stronger than women. Almost in all walks of life, men are dominating in all countries: in the economic and political life, the army and military life, representation, judiciary, the executive branch of government and others. Women feel threatened from men legally, economically, politically and culturally. They are subjected to discrimination. (9) Often, they are raped not only metaphorically but also physically. In some countries women are forced to marry men who they do not know, want or love. All these conditions and circumstances have greatly contributed to sending women into frustration, anger, resentment, bitterness, estrangement and exile metaphorically or physically. Sometimes a wife escapes from a husband because of mistreatment. Women's bitterness at and alienation from men's oppression in certain conditions and places are a familiar example of internalized exile. (10) All these forms of exile have certainly adversely affected the processes of the development of harmonious relations and national cohesion in many countries. (11)

Traditionalism

In all societies there is a degree of traditionalism or conservatism in the cultural and political fields. In more traditional and conservative societies, there is a more pronounced presence in inter-individual and inter-group relations of habits and practices such as intellectual and behavioral restrictions, conformity to group behavior, respect for more rigid social, political and religious hierarchy, a more rigid value and moral order of veneration, preferences and priorities. (12) With these practices in such societies, a lesser amount of freedom, taking of initiative, creation and innovation, expression of individual identity and of self is left for the individual. This state of affairs has positioned many individuals in a physical, emotional and intellectual estrangement, disconnectedness, uprootedness or homelessness.

It is obvious that social and cultural conditions have a restrictive effect on individual and collective development. As a state of exile provides a larger space with less restriction and more freedom, then this kind of development would be expedited and helped by the state of exile.

Colonialism

Colonizing states were a strong force that brought about states of exile for many individuals in the colonized countries. Colonizing states have projected an image of democracy in the social and political fields. As a matter of fact, a considerable degree of socio-political democracy is practiced in these states. This democratic image exacerbated the state of exile that was already reigning among many individuals in the countries subjected to colonialism. Being impressed with this image, and escaping from their countries of birth, a considerable number of intellectuals took residence, whether permanent or temporary, in the erstwhile or present colonizing states. Witnessing social, political, economic and psychological environment which some of them construed, rightly or wrongly, as less than democratic, these individuals found themselves victims of two states of exile: one from their country of birth and the other from the country of their choice. (13)

Whereas certain circumstances may place one in a state of physical exile, or one may go into a state of physical exile, the country of exile may position him/her in a political, psychological or emotional exile. He/she might need that country as a place of physical exile, but he might be exiled from it psychological and politically. This condition places him in at least two states of exile: a physical—and, perhaps, other kinds of—exile from his country of birth, and a political or psychological exile from the country to which he is physically exiled.

Globalization and Maintenance of Identity

Cultural belonging gives identity to the human being. Identity is the conscious and unconscious moral, behavioral, attitudinal, psychological and cultural attributes that define one's identity. As extraordinarily powerful transnational bodies control mechanisms, cultural invasion and globalization have weakened cultural identity. (14) By competing with indigenous cultures, cultural invasion and globalization that carry new and unfamiliar ideas weaken these cultures. Exercise of control has been one of the major factors that enable indigenous cultures to maintain themselves. With their weakening or stripping indigenous cultures of their regulatory control, cultural invasion and globalization have been able to superimpose themselves on the indigenous cultures. (15) As indigenous culture is a major factor in shaping and maintaining the interrelated cultural identity, with the weakening or obliterating of the indigenous culture, the cultural identity has been much weakened. Weakened or eliminated cultural identity for individuals and groups mean that they are thrown into alienation, estrangement and other forms of exile.

Condition of Exile and of Otherness

As has already been pointed out, because of the dynamic mutual influence among the many factors that creates a state of exile and a state of at-homeness and because of the dynamic influence between these factors and the person involved, there is no stable state of exile and of at-homeness. Because of these two types of influence, a sense of full belonging to home and of full state of exile is ideal. If one escapes from many characters of at-homeness, say, from his/her individual and collective memory, from his cultural background, from the symbols of the home, from his cultural reality, and if one feels he/she is estranged to them morally, intellectually, emotionally and culturally, and if there is nothing much left in his/her existence that makes him/her sense a condition of belonging to a home, then, this is an extreme and probably ideal case. In this case, he ceases to be himself and enters a condition of otherness.

Relativity of State of Exile and Creativity

Relativity of state of exile has a positive effect on creativity. Creativity and innovation are not manifested, brought about or nurtured by a linear, even and non-provocative intellectual and emotional setting as much as they are manifested, brought about and nurtured by qualities of non-linearity, unevenness and provocation. Being relative, conditions of states of physical and mental exile better lend themselves to the qualities needed for creativity and innovation.

As creativity involves change, rift or rupture in the social, cultural, political or psychological fields, then a state of exile, which denotes a sort of rift or rupture, is a place of creativity. A rupture is a prerequisite for creativity. There is no creativity without a certain rupture or rift between the self and the psychological, cultural or intellectual environment. The state of exile itself is a site of inspiration, emancipation and creativity. Liminality and marginality make possible new expressions of creativity.

Absence of Full State of Exile

Even though we have conceptualized various forms of exile as indicating lack of belonging, there is, even in these conditions, a certain sense, on the part of the individual, of belonging or connection to that abandoned "home" or a place from which one escaped. (16) This certain sense of belonging or connectedness is the reason, or one of the reasons, for entering the state of exile and for the sense of disconnectedness. The condition of voluntary exile is a function of an unde-clared, denied or hidden, but enduring and surviving, sense of connectedness. (17) It is that existing sense that is seated deep, deep in our conscience. The con-dition of voluntary exile emerged because of the existence of the human sense of connectedness to a place that is claimed as abandoned.

Endnotes

1. Leong Yew, "Exile," Political Discourses—Theories of Colonialism and Postcolonialism, March 8, 2002, p. 2; C. G. Jung, Modern Man in Search of a Soul (San Diego: Harcourt, Brace and Jovanovich, 1933), pp. 197-200; Ronald V. Urick, Alienation: Individual or Social Problem? (Englewood Cliffs, NJ: Prentice-Hall, 1970), p. 7.

2. For inter-action theory, see Paul Meadows, The Many Faces of Change: Explorations in the Theory of Social Change (Cambridge, MA: Schenkman, 1971), pp. 109-27, especially the section on "The Cultural Systems Approach," pp. 128-33.

3. Harold D. Lasswell, Politics: Who Gets What, When, How (New York: Meridian, 1971), p. 13.

4. Salma Khadra Jayyusi, ed., Anthology of Modern Palestinian Literature (New York: Columbia University Press, 1992), pp. 4-5.

5. See, for example, Anna Smith, Julia Kristeva: Readings of Exile and Estrangement (Macmillan, 1996).

6. See, for example, Kerby Miller, Emigrants and Exiles: Ireland and the Irish Exodus to North America (Oxford University Press, 1988; Ashis Nandy, Exiled at Home: Comprising at the Edge of Psychology, the Intimate Enemy and Creating a Nationality (Oxford University Press, 1998).

7. Jayyusi, op. cit., p. 2.

8. Martin Jay, Permanent Exiles: Essays on the Intellectual Migration from Germany to America (Cambridge University Press, 1990).

9. John Dassin, ed., Torture in Brazil. Translated by Jaime Wright (New York: Vintage, 1986), pp. 25-32.

10. Fauziya Kassindja and Layli Miller Bashir, <u>Do They Hear You When You Cry</u> (New York: Delta, 1998). About Simone de Beauvoir's views on the maltreatment of women, see Ian P. McGreal, ed., <u>Great Thinkers of the Western World</u> (New York: Harper Collins, 1992), pp. 546-48.

11. Bell Hooks, <u>Sisters of the Yam</u> (Boston, MA: South End Press, 1993).

12. William Kornblum, <u>Sociology in a Changing World</u> (New York: Holt, Rinehart and Winston, 1988), pp. 207-14.

13. See Renate Siebert, <u>Frantz Fanon: Colonialism and Alienation</u> (New Yoek: Monthly Review Press, 1974).

14. Charles K. Wilber, "Globalization and democracy," in <u>Journal of Economic Issues</u>, Vol.XXXII, No. 2, June 1998, pp. 468-70.

15. Geoff Mulgan, <u>Connexity: How to Live in a Connected World</u> (Boston, MA: Harvard Business School Press, 1997), pp. 19-30.

16. Amin Maalouf, <u>In the Name of Identity</u>. Translated from the French by Barbara Bray. (New York: Arcade, 2000), pp. 1-5.

17. See Benjamin Graves, "Edward W. Said's "Liminal Intellectual," <u>Political Discourse—Theories of Colonialism and Postcolonialism</u>, 1998, p. 1.

* The article was published in <u>Dahesh Voice</u>, Vol. 9, No. 3, Winter 2004.

978-0-595-41243-3
0-595-41243-2

www.ingramcontent.com/pod-product-compliance
Lightning Source LLC
Chambersburg PA
CBHW020428290526
45785CB00002B/745